COURAGE TO SPARKLE:

The Audacious Girls' Guide to Creating a Life that Lights You Up

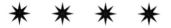

by Lois Barth

Motivational PRESS®
LEADERS IN GLOBAL PUBLISHING

Published by Motivational Press, Inc.
1777 Aurora Road
Melbourne, Florida, 32935
www.MotivationalPress.com

Manufactured in the United States of America.

ISBN: 978-1-62865-305-2

CONTENTS

DEDICATION..5

ACKNOWLEDGMENTS.................................6

INTRODUCTION.......................................9
HOW I FOUND MY COURAGE TO SPARKLE

GEM 1...20
MINING FOR YOUR SPARKLE

GEM 2..30
DON'T BACKBURNER THE BRIGHT LIGHT THAT IS YOU!

GEM 3..44
LET YOUR AUDACIOUS SELF SHINE THROUGH

GEM 4..58
BRING YOUR DARKNESS INTO THE LIGHT

GEM 5..76
LIGHTEN UP WHILE YOU LEARN

GEM 6..88
ILLUMINATING YOUR UNIQUE WIRING

GEM 7...114
FIRE YOUR PERFECTIONIST4

GEM 8...137
HOW TO SHINE IN YOUR CAREER

GEM 9 166
FROM DIMMERS TO SHIMMERS

GEM 10 193
CREATING YOUR SCINTILLATING CIRCLE OF SUPPORT

GEM 11 209
COMMUNICATION THAT GLISTENS

GEM 12 227
THE 5CS OF CREATING A LIFE THAT LIGHTS YOU UP

AFTERWORD 255
COURAGE TO SPARKLE—IT'S A MOVEMENT

ABOUT THE AUTHOR 259

COURAGE TO SPARKLE RESOURCES 261

DEDICATION

✳ ✳ ✳ ✳

For my parents, Ben and Edie, who were the embodiment of the 3L's of an inspired life; learning, loving, and laughter. Their commitment to all three were demonstrated daily in their marriage and their parenting. Both their passion in viewing life as the ultimate classroom in which to grow, and their deep interest in elevating those around them is what stands as their legacy. While they are no longer on the physical plane, they will remain with me always.

ACKNOWLEDGMENTS

✳ ✳ ✳ ✳

I never expected writing a book to be such a rewarding yet contradictory experience. Even though I was alone for hours on end, I rarely felt lonely because I was in the world of my book, and in a large part, I have my Possibility Posse of committed readers to thank for that. My tribe would cheer me on to "keep going!" and spend hours providing me with loving and honest feedback. Enthusiastic comments in my margins like "I need to hear this," and "can't wait to buy a copy for all my girlfriends," kept me going on those days where as an author I truly internalized the lesson that "Writing is rewriting." Heartfelt thanks go to my readers: Richard Damien, Nancy Sheehan, and Deanne Wenger. Special shout-outs to: Katie Carrol-Whitton, Ilona Chessid, Victoria Hart, Kathleen Leuba, and Lisa Weiss.

I'd like Justin Sachs at Motivational Press for reaching out to me with his interest, encouragement, and support in my writing my book. I'd also like to thank the design team at Motivational Press for creating the cover that literally sparkled, and made me smile and realize that my book was really coming to fruition.

Huge buckets of hugs and gratitude to literary midwives Lee Kottner and Victoria Rowan. You both brought your razor sharp eyes, aligned vision and big hearts to the final "push" to create my personal growth meets professional development empowerment go-to-guide for the Audacious Girl; all in a two month period. I will always be grateful to you both, plus we laughed a lot!

To my Sacred Circle of dear friends and family whose continued love and support has made the writing of this book and my life far richer and more rewarding experience: Steve Barth, Elizabeth Browning, Katie Carrol-Whitton, Richard Damien, Patty and Kim DeVoe, Victoria Hart, Peggy Klaus, Kathleen Leuba, Shivaun Mahoney, Paul Levinson, Judith Peterson, Charles Pollak, Carol Rial, Victoria Rowan, Aleta St. James, Karol Ward, and Leigh Williams.

Thanks to Tali and Ophi Edut aka Astro Twins for their SPARKLE-SISTA inspiration and support of my work on so many levels. A special shout out to Jane Rohman and "the team", Johnny Paolillo, and to Anne Twomey for her creative input. Thanks to Natalie Tirrell, a total stranger at the time, (now friend) who went above and beyond to ensure my getting permission to use Portia Nelson's piece, "Autobiograhy in Five Small Chapters."

I am grateful for the opportunity to have Grace Insitute as my non-profit partner, an organization deeply committed to seeing women for the jewels they are and giving them the encouragement and skill set to shine brightly in the world. I continue to be inspired by the work that they do.

I am forever grateful to all the terrific groups and clients I get to speak to and work with. They bring me their most precious resources; their hopes, their vulnerabilities and their dreams. I consider it a supreme honor and a privilege to do this work and their stories and journey have both influenced this book and have provided me with bottomless joy and fulfillment in my life.

Finally I must acknowledge you, dear readers, who desire to stand out, to radiate your brilliance and to celebrate your multi-faceted fabulous selves. Thanks for going on this adventure with me for your Courage to SPARKLE.

Now I can't wait to hear all your sparkle stories...!

INTRODUCTION

✳ ✳ ✳ ✳

HOW I FOUND MY COURAGE TO SPARKLE

✳ **LOIS-ism[1]**

It don't mean a thing...if it ain't got that bling!

One day around my fiftieth birthday, I opened my mailbox and there were two letters. One was an acceptance letter from the college where I had applied to finish my undergraduate degree, and the other was an application for AARP.

"American Association of *Retired* Persons...Retired!" I said out loud to myself. "I've just begun!" I flung my AARP application into the recycling bin, and started college the following week.

Completing my bachelor's degree was my deep longing and dirty little secret, all packed into one. There was no good reason "on paper" to get my degree. I've completed five coaching certifications, read hundreds of books on both personal growth and professional development and became a licensed medical massage therapist. In addition I have had a successful coaching practice for many years, speak regularly and suffice to say, I'm respected in my professional life.

---

1 Lessons, Opportunities Insights and Solutions

Yet when a close friend asked me, "What do you want for your 50th?" I blurted out, "To get my degree," I surprised myself by immediately choking up. In that moment, conviction landed like never before, and I knew that it was time to return to college.

Not everyone thought this was a great idea. My mom, who hovered over me for years after I dropped out of college to pursue an acting career, begged me, "Lo, please finish that degree of yours, you're so smart," now said, "Oh, honey, it's so many years later, why bother?"

I know I'm not alone in my process. I hear it with my clients, my colleagues, and the groups I speak to. We all have these "incompletions" in our lives, goals and dreams that for a number of reasons we either start but never finish or avoid entirely. In some cases it may be a project that is dear to our heart, that we never give it the full attention and focus that it deserves.

Lucky for us, those deep hungers and longings don't go away. We are divinely haunted by our desires. In doing so, they assist us in addressing our internal resistance that counters "Why bother?" with "Because I really want to!" They are our spiritual antennae, beckoning us to move past the stuck and stagnant places in our lives in service of what we only dream may be possible for us. When we take those steps, however big or small, frantic or totally trusting the process, this is all part of the Courage to SPARKLE (C2S).

I knew I would attend Empire State College, part of the State University of New York (SUNY) system. I was drawn to their Adult Learning Model (ALM) that catered to older students who were already accomplished, had worked in their chosen profession for awhile, and needed a flexible schedule in order to work their education into their over-scheduled lives. In addition, they treated you like a grown-up. My graduating class spanned in age from late-twenties to late-eighties; for real! From day one of class, I knew in my heart I had made the right decision. I learned the power of finding your tribe and being part of an academic culture that totally gets who you are and supports it.

In addition to the rigorous course work, I wrote eight essays totaling 120 pages with documentation chronicling what I had learned in my profession and how it contributed to my expertise. I then had follow-up interviews/conversations with different professors where I expanded on the information and insights that I had presented. Out of our dialogue and the material presented, I was awarded a certain amount of credits. While the entire process was quite intensive and rewarding, I wasn't prepared for was how much that journey would change me.

I felt as if I had traveled back in time to revisit my prior body of work as a coach, speaker, actress, comedienne, arts educator, and massage therapist. In addition, I had to reach out to people I had worked with up to twenty years earlier in order to provide proof of our work together. I felt excited to reconnect with them even though a small part of me was a bit embarrassed and ashamed about my "incompletion," and had a giant case of the "what ifs?" *What if* they thought my goal was too small or too pedestrian? *What if* they asked why I had dropped out of two very good colleges, especially given the fact that I did quite well in high school and came from a stable and loving middle-class family? *What if* they asked me what stopped me from finishing my degree when I was more "age appropriate?"

I see how easy it is to "what if" ourselves out of taking the necessary risks and actions in service of living our most vibrant selves? I took a deep breath, "smiled and dialed," and one by one, reached out to people and institutions from my past.

I was quickly reminded of what I often find to be true in life: that our worst fears rarely materialize. Instead of criticizing or judging, everyone I spoke to could not have been more supportive and helpful. Whether it was a simple "good for you" or a heartfelt conversation, in one way or another, everyone echoed both words of encouragement and deep respect for what I was doing. My previous "dirty little secret" was now, simply, a deep longing being fulfilled. The experience was transformative for me.

Fast-forward two years later: I was two months away from graduation and I heard that three students would be selected to speak at the graduation. I laughed to myself, "Wouldn't it be ironic to speak in front of 600 people about something I avoided talking about for three decades?" The competition was pretty tight, but figuring I had nothing to lose, I went for it. I was one of the three students selected and the only woman.

I shared the ironic journey of my "dirty little secret" being transformed into a proud accomplishment with my graduating class. As I shared the lessons learned by completing my degree, I saw the nodding heads of fellow travelers on the road-less-traveled college degree path.

My eighty-four-year-old mother who had previously said, "Why bother?" was now beaming and all dolled up with her wildly crepe paper-decorated walker with a helium balloon attached that said, "Congratulations, Graduate!"

The very first thing I did when I received my diploma in the mail was to go on to LinkedIn, that pesky little site that bugged me regularly with its default prompt that was, to me, an ominous question: "Degree?" For years I'd click, "close window." Now, I could finally type in, "Yes!" "What kind of degree?" the software asked. "Bachelors in Human Development." "Year?" I said out loud, "None of your damn business!"

I am constantly tickled by how the universe sends us cosmic validations. A few months later, I was speaking at a large organization about the "Courage to SPARKLE," which puts equal emphasis on what makes us feel most alive and engaged in our lives as well as strategically addressing our resistances and moving through them. At the end of my keynote, a woman in her sixties in a C-Suite position at a top investment firm took me aside. In a quiet voice—and not knowing my own educational history—said, "Something shifted for me today. It's crazy. I'm five years away from retiring. It has nothing to do with my current position, but I want to go back for my undergraduate degree."

Even though she was well-respected and had 200 people reporting to her, she held that unfulfilled goal as a deep dark secret as well. I shared my journey with her about my degree and she lit up. She added that one of her regrets of starting a family so young was opting out of getting her degree. Now, several decades later and five years away from retirement, she thought it would be an ideal way to both finish a chapter in her life while starting a new one.

The more I shared my college story with people, the more they revealed some of their own unmet dreams, regrets, or desires to feel more authentic and self-expressed in their lives. The more I expressed my Audacious Self—transparent, vulnerable, playful, and even outrageous—the more I automatically gave permission for others to do the same. That's the way it works.

Then it occurred to me, how similar we all are. We may think we project these got-it-all-together exteriors, but that doesn't mean inside we still don't hunger to heal the scared and wounded places that we know stop us from living our most vibrant lives. We crave to have deeply intimate and connected relationships; to create a life that lights us up. Not a life that someone else told us we should live, but one that we feel truly engaged in. We're looking for the "Courage to SPARKLE."

What's all this SPARKLE about?

I wear lots and lots of bling-bling wherever I go. I always have. I'm sure I'll be one of those ninety-year-old ladies with matchy-matchy bling-bling outfits. I don't care if it's not in style at the time. I'm a SPARKLE-Sista; it's who I am!

My love affair with SPARKLE began with my parents. My dad was a world-traveler for business and pleasure. He never traveled like a tourist or a typical businessman. I remember once when he and my Mom returned from Morocco. We'd turned the dining room lights up to 11 and spread their travel loot out on the table. They'd brought home three amazing necklaces for my sister and I. One was made of sterling silver and had letters engraved in it with silver bells, another one was a mosaic made of different colored glass, and a third was encrusted with semi-precious stones. I'd wear them *everywhere*. You know the expression, "I'll be there with bells on?" Well, I actually was!

My mom always encouraged me to wear jewelry nobody else had, to stand out, to be one-of-a-kind. In my fourth grade school pictures, almost every little girl wore a version of a frilly dress with a dainty locket; not me. There I was with a Moroccan perfume holder from the eighteenth century around my neck. While other kids wore baby bracelets and little stud earrings, I wore huge medallions the size of most kids' wrists. I didn't know anything different, because my childhood home was filled with antiques and off-beat furnishings. I was encouraged to express what was different about me. My friends would ask to try on and play with my jewelry. By being self-expressed in even something as basic as my jewelry and clothing, I now see I gave my friends permission to *try on* what self-expression would feel like for them. That is really what the Courage to SPARKLE is all about.

My family is one of big personalities. Like all families, we have our quirks but love to laugh about them. It wasn't unusual for me as a young girl to dance in front of the living room mirror that covered the entire wall or to sing a show tune while putting the clothes out to dry on the laundry line. I loved meeting new people and learning about their lives.

My mom would have in-depth conversations on a regular basis with everyone from the garbage man to the mailman. While at the time I would feel impatient, I learned from her that everyone has a story, and embedded in those stories are both messages and lessons of enormous value. My mother's goal was always to entertain and make people feel loved and special.

Thanks to these influences, I had the Courage to SPARKLE. It felt natural to who I was. I'm sure that many of you can remember feeling free to be however you wanted as a child.

Then, like many of us, I lost my SPARKLE. I went on Dimmers, which is when I feel disconnected from my aliveness and vitality. My spirit becomes dull. The first time I remember being on Dimmers was when I was around twelve. I had lost my

BFF to a mean-spirited girl, who not only took her away from me but gained vicarious pleasure from tormenting and humiliating me. I learned first-hand the traumatic nature of being bullied.

She used the very thing I celebrated, my excitement for life, my uniqueness, and bigger-than-life personality as fodder to torture me. Several of the other kids joined in. I suddenly became too concerned with what people thought of me. Instead of enjoying what made me different, I felt like an outsider and isolated. Being an exceedingly sensitive and at times, intensely emotionally person, I told myself I was too weird, too intense, *too much*. I now see that my experience of being "too much" is really first cousins to feeling *not good enough*.

We all have our own version of being on Dimmers. When I ask people to look at their earlier childhood, they can usually pinpoint where a core fragment of their most authentic self starts to split off. It often shows up when they look at old childhood pictures and they see it; a frozen smile, or a dullness in the eye, or not-so-subtle closed-off body language.

To a greater or lesser extent, we've all gotten tossed around in this big beautiful mess called life. I questioned my value, struggled with second-guessing myself, and sacrificed my unique SPARKLE on the altar of perfectionism. As a result, my spirit dimmed. I plummeted. Soon, I was drowning in a sea of self-loathing and had a wicked eating disorder. My romantic relationships were one train wreck after another.

By the time I was twenty-two, I had dropped out of two excellent colleges, moved around New York City eleven times in twenty-six months. I worked multiple jobs as a waitress, coat check, bagel vendor, ice cream server, and ridiculous office jobs that used none of my interests, talents, abilities, or gifts. My shortest tenure in the employment world was working three hours as "the worst food-processor demonstrator that ever set foot in Macy's cellar"—a coveted honor since my competition was fierce.

I also had the wonderful adventures of interesting and rewarding acting jobs, studying clowning in Italy, and going undercover and working the party circuit through a vast array of full-body costumes: as a gorilla delivering singing telegrams with a Mae West accent, Barney, a Christmas Tree, a nearsighted Dancing Bear, an oversized Girl Scout, and a voluptuous Elf. I impersonated Dolly Parton, Bette Midler and Barbra Streisand while wearing what is called *Big Heads* — humongous, papier-mâché heads that are caricatures of celebrities — that are dark, sweaty, and warp sound so you feel like you're in an echo chamber.

But no matter what was happening in my life, no matter how far away I felt from my dreams or how disconnected from my true self, I've always had this passionate curiosity about how we grow and evolve as human beings. A gift I now see that I received from my parents. I have always known, on a certain level, that I am enrolled in the classroom of life. Each day—no matter what I'm feeling, or my experiences, whether pleasant or not—contains within it a series of life lessons. By looking for the lessons and the messages within them, we are encouraged to try things on, or throw things out. In so doing, we have the opportunity to thrive.

A few years ago, I wasn't feeling well. While I was resting in bed, I looked up at my bling-bling bureau. Yes, I have an entire bureau filled with bling-bling. I took a good look and realized the universe, yet again, was talking to me. I was listening! I looked at each piece of my bling-bling, and I noticed how each one was so unique and sparkled in its own right.

I realized how closely my collection mirrored us as human beings: the ability to stand out, shimmer its light, and to celebrate the variety of creative potential. Like each piece of my jewelry, we are all multi-faceted. We are not simply our jobs or our personalities, even though these elements make up our lives. We are so much more.

Taking the time to consider how we're uniquely wired, what makes us feel alive and vibrant and honoring our hopes and dreams in an ongoing way—that, my friends, is exactly what this book is about: The *Courage to SPARKLE*.

I adore my bling-bling and always find myself drawn *to things* that SPARKLE. I have come to realize that what really inspires me most are *people* who SPARKLE; who stand out, radiate their goodness and passion in the world and celebrate all of who they are. My life's calling is to support others to cultivate their own SPARKLE. I know that in doing so, I'll be nurturing my own.

How to Use This Book

Here's where my twelve Gems come in. These Gems cover the different areas of life and contain within them principles and techniques. These foundational elements have been instrumental in supporting others (and myself!) in having successful relationships, building businesses, health goals, career transitions, and generally making life a lot lighter and light-filled in every way. In addition, throughout these Gems, I have included my LOIS-isms (Lessons, Opportunities, Insights and Solutions)—my favorite time-tested wisdom nuggets.

Here's the thing: Feel free to read this book as a dipper or a diver—both ways work! Go ahead, dip into those few Gems that seem most relevant and immediate to you. Others of you may be divers, you will be most likely to go through this book Gem by Gem, do all the exercises, download my C2S Workbook,[2] reference my SMART SEXY TV episodes, and have more text highlighted than not. You too will be rewarded!

So, thanks for picking up my jewel-box. I couldn't be happier to share my favorite gems with you. May you laugh with recognition, shed tears of healing, get excited by what's possible for you, and act on what lights you up. Most of all, may you have the Courage to SPARKLE.

---

2 http://www.loisbarth.org/workbook.html

GEM 1

✳ ✳ ✳ ✳

MINING FOR YOUR SPARKLE

When I talk about the Courage to SPARKLE, people have the most interesting responses. They laugh, smile, make surprised, and thoughtful sounds like "Hhhhhh," and "Mmmm."

And "Wooooowwww."

Recently I was on a date, where the guy flung himself back in his chair and howled, "Awwwwwwwwww!" followed by, 'Courage to SPARKLE' that's visceral! I'm not even sure what it means, but it sounds amazing!"

He's right; Courage to SPARKLE is visceral. It starts at the core of your being.

We're in an interesting era of history, deeply affected by technology and the seismic changes we're undergoing as a culture and society on the whole. That line from the TV commercial, "That was so thirty-eight seconds ago!" is more true than ever before. There are enormous options and choices available to us to fill out time and take our focus. It's easy to fall into the mode of piling more information and activities on our metaphoric plate, over stimulating ourselves with images, busyness with no time to really digest or inquiry what we find fulfilling or holds meaning for us. As a result it's easy to creating a culture of feeling overfed yet being undernourished.

I hear this exact complaint from my clients and groups—I see it in my own life, if I'm not careful—the stress, deep feelings of isolation, exhaustion, and not feeling fulfilled even though "on paper" they may have these great lives. By taking the time to slow down, reflect, and really look at what the Courage to SPARKLE looks like for *you,* not what you think it *should* look and feel like but what is true for you, you'll learn to nourish your best self.

Speaking clients hire me often saying, "We need some light entertainment and some great motivational tips." While I deliver that, they quickly realize that my work goes much deeper.

When I work with large audiences, I break the participants into small groups to share what their C2S looks like. I see four reactions simultaneously. Most will get all animated when they talk about what makes them SPARKLE. Then they are pleasantly surprised to learn what makes their colleagues SPARKLE as well. Some tear up when they realize how disconnected they are from their SPARKLE, and most poignantly, others will stare off into space totally stumped by the question, "What does makes me SPARKLE?"

I see this introspection as a wonderful opportunity to dive into the truths of your life. My invitation for you is to take a deep breath, to be wildly curious and really ask yourself, "What makes me SPARKLE? What does my SPARKLE look and feel like?" That's what this Gem is all about.

What Your SPARKLE Is—And Isn't:

"I'm good at doing a lot of things, but is that what makes me SPARKLE?" I get this question a lot. The answer is "yes," "no," and "it depends."

Yes. I would say the answer is "yes" when what you do on a regular basis delights you, and you feel that shimmer of energy and fulfillment in your life. Identifying one's SPARKLE is more about how you feel about what you do rather than just what you do.

For example, one of my former clients, Kaitlin[3], is in banking. She's a "yes" to her SPARKLE when she is forging strategic partnerships, and doing deeply intensive "people-centric" activities that are about relationship building. She feels alive, engaged, and rewarded, even when it's demanding and challenging. Being a relationship-oriented person, she's constantly bringing this piece of her SPARKLE to her personal life as well.

No. Part of her job is also doing very technical work that revolves around projections, multi-tab complex spreadsheets, and lots of politics. Is she good at it? Yes. Does it light her up? No! She doesn't hate it or dread it, but it's not part of her SPARKLE. I will go into greater detail later in this Gem about how to separate skill sets from SPARKLE, but you're getting the picture.

It Depends. What makes us SPARKLE depends on how it engages our spirit and creates vitality in our lives. It also often changes, depending on what juncture we're at in our lives. For instance, I have worked with women who truly felt the SPARKLE when their kids were younger. It didn't mean it wasn't hard at times. Yet once their lovely little ones turned into teenagers, they feel a resounding "NNNNOOOOOOOOO!" in terms of parenting being a source of their SPARKLE.

---

3   All client names have been changed to preserve anonymity. Others' stories are used in the text under their real names by permission.

Does that mean they're going to quit their "Mom" job? Hopefully not. They do, however, need to address what different ways they'll connect with their SPARKLE that supports their parenting role at this challenging juncture. As a result, their aliveness will spill over into other areas. That's why tuning in on a semi-regular basis and doing, what I call, a "SPARKLE check-in" is so critical.

Three Ps of Clarifying Your SPARKLE

Feel free to download your C2S Workbook[4], and answer the following questions. Don't overthink it. You can always go back later and review.

Passions

* What are the activities, projects, or people you find your-self naturally drawn to and feel passionate about (e.g., hobbies, subjects, tasks, particular people you spend time with personal and professional)?
* Why (e.g., putting on parties provides a sense of community, fun, and creativity)?
* What are the top three things you'd do if you never needed to work again (e.g., travel, volunteer, take classes)?
* Why (e.g., I'm fascinated by other cultures, I love making a difference and learning)?

Any themes emerging (e.g., I feel most passionate when I'm around people, learning new things and being creative.)?

---

4   http://www.loisbarth.org/workbook.html

Pet Peeves

As women, we often get messages that it's bad to feel or express our anger, but we also help perpetuate the taboo against anger by trying to reason ourselves out of it. Or, we go the other way completely and repress it. Then, when we can't take it anymore, we may express it in very aggressive and ineffective ways. I know I definitely have done all three.

Obviously, a steady diet of getting irritated and enraged leaves you stressed out and not fun to be around. At times, it is important to get perspective and "not to sweat the small stuff."

There's also enormous value in getting interested in what irritates us (Pet Peeves), all the way to what outright enrages us. Contained within both are core messages about our values. These "irritants" are often associated with the things we believe in most and are most passionate about in our lives. If you can figure out how these irritations inform your values, and incorporate that knowledge into your life, you'll be making a major shift in feeling more aligned with your most authentic self.

An example in my own life is that I abhor waste of any kind; food, money, time and worst of all, human potential. When I see large bags of food being thrown out, my heart breaks, I can't help thinking of someone two miles away that may be going to bed hungry. Last week, I was at a dinner with a new friend and she left over most of her meal on her plate. When she declined to take it home, I jumped in and said, "I will! I'm sure there's someone outside who would love to eat such a lovely salad." I laughed at first, a tad embarrassed that I blurted it out so quickly without really knowing her, but she was delighted. When I found a taker, it created a bond between us and we felt better.

When I'm being put on hold for a half-hour and forced to listen to a recording that "your business matters to us," I'm irritated that my time is being wasted even though I attempt to get other stuff done at the same time. The worst is when I see really smart, kind people wasting their value by pursuing relationships with toxic people. I hate it.

This irritation/full-blown source of being enraged reminds me of my core values: effectivity, kindness, generosity, and fulfillment. Having a strong sense of these core values behind my irritation directs the people I choose to have in my life, the activities I engage in, and the type of work I pursue. It's enormously freeing for me, and can be for you, too.

I'm rigorous with my clients to make sure they use their most precious resources of time, energy, and money in ways that will support their personal and professional goals.

You can use the following exercises to help determine what irritates you, and what that says about your core values. Go back to your C2S Workbook and answer the following questions in as much detail as you feel you need to. If you're inspired, keep going.

* Name three things that irritate you (e.g., unconscious driving in parking lots, texting while walking).

* Why (e.g., not considering others' needs, unaware of selfish behavior)?

* Name three things that completely *enrage* you (e.g., people who bully or manipulate vulnerable people).

* Why (e.g., it's unfair, cruel and dangerous)?

* If you could head up your own campaign to eradicate one thing you feel super irritated by what would that be (e.g., a no-tolerance campaign toward mean and nasty behavior)?

(You can do this exercise over and over, so just pick the first thing that comes to you.)

* What would your bumper sticker or motto be (e.g., Want to Change the World? Be Kind!)?

* Why that campaign (e.g., when we have a world of kindness, we will be in a better place to address many issues)?

* How do your Pet Peeves reveal your core values (e.g., compassion, thoughtfulness contribution, communication, generosity, tolerance, and of course-kindness)?

* How can you express them more in your life in a way that makes you SPARKLE (e.g., create a Gem of a Person monthly campaign at work where a team member gets publicly acknowledged for the specific ways they've delivered exceptional work)?

What are the overall takeaways from the Pet Peeve section of the 3Ps? (e.g., I need to take more actions to attract supportive and generous people in both my personal and professional life).

Purpose

When we feel connected to our life's purpose, consciously or unconsciously, we are both expressing specific qualities, which I call *Being*, and taking particular actions or displaying specific skills, something I refer to as *Doing*. I believe it's really essential to look at life purpose from both the *Being* and *Doing* vantage points because, both are equally important.

Let me give you a specific example. A friend of mine is a dentist and he loves it, which is really unusual since it's one of the most stressful jobs out there. Being a dentist gives him a chance to express his life's purpose every day.

On a practical level, he fills cavities, and makes crowns and flawless veneers. The *Doing* part of his job involves critical thinking, mechanical work with his hands, and a deep expertise in anatomy and, of course, dentistry. While he enjoys the intellectual and physical part of his job, if that's all he did, he'd be bored out of his mind. That's because those skills, even though he's superb at it, do not fall within his life purpose.

That's where the *Being* part of his life's purpose comes in, which is his desire to inspire, entertain, and teach people. Family and friends send him jokes from all over the world and he can't wait to share them with his patients who come in and say "Hey, Doc, it's been a stressful day, you got a joke for me?"

Patients often share their woes with him, and he delights in sharing a story that may brighten them up or give them the ability to shift their perspective. In addition, he finds it rewarding to work with deeply phobic patients by helping them transform their fear of dentistry. It intersects with his life purpose, which is to inspire and teach.

Here are, perhaps, some examples from your own life:

Doing	Being
Solving problems	Reflective, Analytical, Strategic
Providing a sounding board	Patient, Present, Kind, Loving
Connecting friends with cool people.	Social, Adventurous, Innovative

While there's clearly an overlap at times, my clients find it really powerful to tease out the *Being* and the *Doing* part of their life purpose, since it is a very individual process. Here are some questions that can help you do that.

Name three experiences that you have felt most aligned with your purpose in your life? Rather than writing down "when I help people," be specific. Some examples may be:

* Ability to break down projects into small action items.
* Asking them helpful questions so they can draw their own conclusions.
* Connecting them with cool restaurants and activities.

When looking at life purpose, it's really easy to think of it as some kind of mythic undertaking that has to look bigger than life. Don't put that pressure on yourself. It can be very simple like, "I feel most connected with my life purpose when I'm inspiring others to see the physical beauty in the world." In this case, *Doing* and *Being* might look like this:

Doing	Being
Making art, filmmaking	Educating
Gardening	Inspiring
Research, outreach, analysis	Advocacy, volunteering, social action

Concrete examples of the manifestation of *Doing* and *Being* could be: "I feel connected with my life purpose when I figure out a problem that not only makes my own life better but the lives of those around me." The more specific you can be the more clarity you'll gain. Rather than what you're good at, or pays the bills, focus on when you feel most aligned and alive. Now, you try.

I feel most connected to my life purpose when I:

Why (e.g., solving problems for myself and others allow us greater freedom and enjoyment in our lives, and I find it deeply gratifying to provide that for them)?

What have you learned about both the *Being* and *Doing* part of your life purpose (e.g., I've learned that the crunching numbers part of my job is my *Doing* but my *Being* is the ability to find ways to save my customers money and reduce their expenses)?

As you go deeper into the 3Ps and pay attention in your life more, you'll start to notice what makes you feel most inspired and energized in your life.

Don't pressure yourself into thinking that everything you do in your professional job has to perfectly align with the 3Ps. You may find, as in the case of my friend the dentist, that while the skill set is vital to doing the work, it may not be a key element of your SPARKLE.

Check-In

* ✴ What did I learn from this Gem?
* ✴ How can I apply it?
* ✴ What small action can I take?

GEM 2

✳ ✳ ✳ ✳

DON'T BACKBURNER THE BRIGHT LIGHT THAT IS YOU!

"Our deepest fear is not that we are inadequate. Our deepest fear is that we are powerful beyond measure. It is our light, not our darkness that most frightens us."

Those opening lines from Marianne Williamson's book, *A Return to Love: Reflections on the Principles of a Course in Miracles,* move me every time I read them. Whenever I share those words during one of my keynotes, I see many women's eyes well up with tears of the resounding truth that they are confronted by sharing their light with the world.

I explore the importance of embracing both our shadows and our lights in greater detail in Gem 4—"Bring Your Darkness into the Light." But suffice to say, when we don't face our fear of living up to our potential, we will continue to put our SPARKLE on hold. I know I certainly did. That was before I discovered that when I stopped putting my SPARKLE on hold, everything changed for the better.

The Day I Stopped "Weight-Listing" My Life

I was twenty-six. For close to a dozen years, I had an eating disorder that decimated my spirit and quality of life. My most dramatic weight swing was when I went from 98-120 to 180 pounds in less than two years, between the ages of fifteen and seventeen. People didn't recognize me, and worst of all, I stopped recognizing myself. I hid out in horrible muumuus and sweatpants. It wasn't unusual for someone to shake their head sadly and say, "So young and pregnant." Mortifying! Most upsetting, I knew I hadn't given birth to my true self! The biggest tragedy was how the focus on my dieting, weight, body, and food eclipsed my optimism, my love of life, my light-heartedness, and my talents I so craved to express. My eating disorder hijacked my life and re-routed me into a very small world: "Once-I'm-Thin Land."

I definitely took actions to escape that world. I went to twelve-step programs, private therapy, spiritual services, and read tons of self-help, dieting, and health-fad books. I believe they were all contributing factors to my spiritual awakening that was the beginning of the end of my eating disorder. The one thing that concretized all my relentless work was the day I stopped "weight-listing" my life. It happened like this:

It's 4:30 p.m. on a gray Wednesday, and I'm leaving my apartment. As I put the key in the door to lock up, my negative self-talk voice that I now call my *Itty Bitty Committee* starts haranguing me with the usual nonsense: "I can't believe what you ate. You'll never be thin. You'll be 180 pounds for the rest of your life." Same old same old, back and forth, ricocheting through the same anxiety-ridden, loopy thinking that kept me stuck.

That day, however, another voice interrupted with a quiet pervasiveness and a kind tone that I couldn't ignore. It said, "What if you could never lose or gain another pound again in your life? How would you live your life?"

Contemplating that nightmare scenario stopped my ricocheting. Whose voice was this? I now see that as the birth of my *Sweetheart Voice*—my compassionate self who reinforces self-love and inner advocacy. I had never heard that voice before so, initially, I was stunned. When I look back, I see all the work that I had been doing on myself was finally seeping through my consciousness in ways I never dreamed possible.

Listening to my *Sweetheart Voice's* guidance, I re-opened my apartment door, took out my scale, and put it in the "one neighbor's junk is another neighbor's cool stuff" pile. I attach a note that reads, "This scale works perfectly, it just no longer works for me. Enjoy!" Then I went back into my apartment and started writing what I called my "Stop Weight-Listing My Life: Things I'll do Once I'm Thin List. The list went something like this:

* Get rid of all my sweatpants, even if they're black.
* Wear clothes that show I have a body and are totally me.
* Wear colors other than black.
* Eat cookies in public.
* Remind myself that nobody died from being told "No."
* Whenever possible, eliminate all mean people from my life.
* Say "No" to men I'm not interested in.
* Flirt with guys who I am attracted to even if I think aren't "in my league."

* Say "Yes" and "No" without explaining why.

* Only have relationships with guys who like my body.

* Buy *that* bathing suit.

* Wear *that* bathing suit. On the beach. Without a cover-up sarong. When others are present. Not care what they think.

* Have adventures regularly.

* Sing on the street regularly and get others to sing along.

* Travel.

* Go to auditions that speak to me, whether I believe I'm ready or not.

* Say "I'm angry" when I'm angry.

* Cry when I'm sad.

* Love myself whether I'm binging or eating right.

* Stop apologizing for being alive.

* Work on telling the truth versus getting people to like me.

* Own a house in the country.

* Earn a living doing things that give me energy vs. those that sap my energy.

* Do stand-up comedy whether I think I'm funny or not.

* Get real. I'm funny!

* Stop putting my dreams on hold.

There were so many things on the list. I kept revising, tweaking, and adding. But I started checking things off my list and that's when the magic happened. Without the wait of losing the weight, I had no more excuses for not living. I had several disappointments along the way.

One example was when I decided to flirt with guys I felt drawn to, even though I considered them *out of my league*. I had previously created this whole story in my head that if I did that, and they weren't interested, I would feel too humiliated to function. It obviously felt nice to have my interest reciprocated and when that happened I was delighted. The really rich moments that contributed to my transformation, however, were when those guys weren't interested. The epiphany that the painful feelings of rejection that I avoided, were not nearly as devastating as I had imagined. Even when faced with disappointment, I was still glad I took the risk.

As I crossed more and more of these previously considered "big deals," action items off my list, and I often found that they were anything *but* big deals, I experienced a fair amount of sadness. Here I had put them and in a sense, my life on hold for so long only to find out how ultimately they were not such big deals. Ultimately, I found it to be a big relief.

Other actions were terrifying, and I shook while I did them, but I did them anyway. The biggest gift was that I was living in my real "warts-and-all" life, not my "one-day-when-I'm-thin-it-will-be-perfect" fantasy life that kept me stuck.

It was amazing what wonderful things started to happen. My life got bigger and my body got smaller. I lost thirty-five pounds in less than four months. I fell in love with a fabulous guy who not only adored my body but loved me. We had adventures, went dancing, and it was the first time that I knew what it was to have a romance with a guy who was truly a friend. I got multiple acting jobs in stand-up comedy, theatre, and even some films. What I discovered over and over was that the more I was "myself," the more I got hired.

I obsessed less about what I was eating and more often asked myself, "What am I really hungry for?" on all levels; emotionally, creatively, spiritually and of course physically. Did I still occasionally binge like crazy? You betcha! But my overeater was playing less and less of a role in my life, because I demoted her from her original role of CPO: Chief Perfectionism Officer. I downsized her with a burgeoning sense of self and excitement for life.

While my list came about as an antidote for my eating disorder, I have yet to meet one person who doesn't have their own way of putting life on hold. I called it a "Weight List," but for others it's a "Wait List" which looks like: "I'm going to *wait* until I *X* so that I can do *Y* and experience *Z*."

LOIS-ism

Common Sense—Uncommonly Practiced

We have it all backwards. Do the damn thing *now*, and watch what shows up in your life!

I'm not talking about your Bucket List, the list of things we are excited to do before we're six feet under. The Bucket List is a dynamic and wonderful list of hopes, dreams, and adventures you're excited about pursuing even if they may be a one-time experience. The Bucket List is something that compels you to move forward. It's rooted in enthusiasm and optimism. On the other hand, the "Wait-Listing List" is about putting your true most essential life on hold based on fear, perfectionism, and fantasy.

The "One day when I'm..." excuse comes up often when I'm coaching clients or speaking to my groups. I call it one of the many great myths that keep our SPARKLE on hold. The challenge is that there are often legitimate reasons why the timing is off or making those changes is inconvenient. Our rationalization is like a little pitbull that just grabbed hold of a giant bone and is chomping away at all the delicious morsels of those legitimate reasons why it's not a good time.

I will discuss the importance of planning and preparation and how that is different from procrastination later on in this Gem, but for now, let's look at:

The Great Family of Myths that Keep Our SPARKLE on HOLD.

THE FAKE FINISH LINE MYTH

The fantasy that if we get "all this stuff done," most of which we may not even want to do, then we'll have time to do the things we want to do most. My friend, Ramone, calls this the "Fake Finish Line." It makes us fritter away our time on things that are less dear to our hearts, or stay up hours past when our bodies are begging us to go to sleep. There is no finish line. Do what makes you SPARKLE now! Don't wait for the fake finish line; it doesn't exist.

WHEN I GET "THERE" MYTH

Nearby to the Fake Finish Line is the big, bad "When I Get There" myth. We won't give ourselves credit until we're "There." We refuse to consider ourselves successful until we're "There." What does "There" even mean? Again, it's another iteration of a fake, imaginary life that keeps you in a state of discontent and refusing to give yourself credit or have gratitude for where you are right now.

There's nothing wrong with having goals and specific bench-marks for what we want to accomplish; every business and pro-fessional development book tells us different ways to do that. Milestones are fine, but "There" is different. To deprive your-self of acknowledging how great your life is right now, or cele-brating what you already have accomplished because you're not "There," means you accomplish nothing. Quit it! And, yes, I have to remind myself of this all the time.

THE DUCKS IN A ROW MYTH

I have a 116-year-old farmhouse in upstate New York. I learn an equal number of lessons while living in my rural surroundings as I do in my urban dwelling. I refer to these lessons as my "Country Curriculum," one of my favorite ones being The "Ducks in a Row" Myth.

In the ten years I have been in this house, I have only seen ducks walk in a row three times. I am here to report that all three times, they did it when they felt like it. Usually at the most inconvenient times in the middle of traffic, which is basically our neighbors who drive pickups and tractors. Every time it happened, it was a shocker. They'd waddle at their own pace, quacking as they took their damn time to cross the road. But once they got to the other side, the row quickly dissolved into mayhem. I timed each ducks-in-a-row crossing and it was never more than ninety seconds.

If we keep the fantasy going that at some point everything will line up in perfect order—aka "Ducks in a Row"—before taking action or moving forward, the outcome is pretty much the same: we're putting our SPARKLE on hold. That *illusion* of order only lasts a very short time before it, too, becomes mayhem. One of my favorite slogan from twelve-step programs is: "You can act your way into good thinking a lot quicker than you can think your way into good action." How true that is!

PLANNING VERSUS PROCRASTINATION

There are times in life when the correct next action is not clear. We must slow down and reconsider where our focus needs to be. That is not the same as procrastinating. That's about preparation and planning. Sometimes we're not ready to do something because it truly doesn't feel like the right timing. Perhaps there is additional preparation and planning necessary before acting on it. Other times we have all these random excuses for not doing what we really know we need to do and I call that "GVR" (garden variety resistance) aka procrastination, how do we know the difference? Check in with yourself to really explore what the fear is, and where you feel stopped.

In the face of GVR or procrastination, if we are honest with ourselves and really look at the reasons that are stopping us, we'll start to see the difference between GVR or that the timing isn't right. Perhaps we need to take some preparatory steps until we are truly ready. When we're resistant, conversely, what is usually at play is deeply seated negative beliefs (e.g., too old, too young, not good enough) and often perfectionism is behind that. When we peel away the layers of beliefs that stop us, what may start as "I don't know enough to do this" becomes a challenge in which we can ask ourselves, "What are the absolute basics that I need to know to at least start the process?" I always find that by staying open and asking for support, we'll discover the steps along the way.

Conversely, there are times when we're legitimately in the "bad timing" category, which is usually less about fear and more about an honest assessment of both priorities and capacity within the context of our lives. For example, one colleague of mine was in the process of changing careers while both sons were in high school. While she was getting a lot of on-the-job training in her new industry, she always planned to get her PhD. She did a lot of research and had concluded that taking this vital step in her education would provide her the expertise, impact, credibility and income that she desired. She reviewed her options and took a hard look at timing. After much review and consideration, she realized that if she opted to enroll in a night program while her boys were still in school, it would make tremendous demands on both her own well-being and possibly her ability to be there for her kids. Assessing both her priorities and the capacity she had, with a clear mind and an open heart, she decided to wait four years until both children went away to college. When the time did come, she immersed herself in a full-time PhD program, started an exciting new chapter in her life, and got a full fellowship. While the program was demanding she felt excited about the ability to fully commit to the program and was confident that she had made the right decision.

There's a big difference between procrastinating and delaying acting on a project because additional planning is needed. The need to assess whether you have the capacity at a certain time in your life to move forward on a project or a goal is a principle I call "Honoring your Emotional and Mental Bandwidth," which I go into far greater depth in Gem 6.

If you're confused as to whether it's a procrastination or a "bad timing" issue, get support. Call a friend or colleague who you feel is equipped to support you, work with a coach or a therapist, or do some mindfulness work like journaling. If you're willing to be honest with yourself, it will quickly become clear what's operating. Once we understand where the resistance is, we have more clues on the best strategies moving forward.

EXERCISES

✳   ✳   ✳   ✳

Exercise 1—Create Your Own "Stop Wait-Listing Your Life" List

Make a list. Write down fifteen to twenty things you've wanted to do but have been putting on hold out of fear and resistance. Don't overthink it. It can include life-long dreams like meeting the love of your life and finding the career of your dreams, and less emotionally charged goals like throwing out the stack of newspapers from six months ago.

After you've written your list:

* Go through each item and check in with your feelings about each one.

* Notice the ones that totally inspire you, and which ones you dread.

* Cross off the "shoulds" and keep the "Wow, that would be great!" items.

* Edit the list down to no more than fifteen to twenty.

* Post it in a high-visibility place like your kitchen or office area.

* Take small but consistent actions to fulfill them one at a time.

* When you cross one off, write what happened as a result.

* Share this concept with a buddy.

* Support each other in making them happen (more on this later).

* Celebrate yourself and the new chapter in your life.

Exercise 2—Dealing with Your Resistance

If you find yourself stuck with a few items on your list that you are still not able to do, answer these questions:

* The reason I'm not doing ⎯⎯⎯⎯⎯ is because of ⎯⎯⎯.

* My concern is that if I do ⎯⎯⎯⎯⎯ then⎯⎯⎯⎯ will happen.

* What is the chance of X really happening?

* What if it did happen?

* How could I handle it?

* What small step can I take to move forward on it?

* How can I get support on it?

* How will I celebrate after taking that action?

* What I learned from this process is:

SUGGESTIONS

* Make it fun.

* Don't overthink it.

* Prioritize Progress over Perfection.

* Do a weekly check-in either on your own or with a support buddy.

* Take a few notes on what is shifting in your life.

* Share it with others.

CHECK-IN

* What did I learn from this Gem?

* How can I apply it?

* What small actions can I take?

GEM 3

✳ ✳ ✳ ✳

LET YOUR AUDACIOUS SELF SHINE THROUGH

Since you've read this far, you most likely belong to the tribe of women who want to shake things up in your lives. You wouldn't have picked up this book with the subtitle, "The Audacious Girl's Guide to Creating a Life that Lights You Up," if you weren't!

Based on what I've seen in my professional practice and personal life, most women are prone to second-guessing themselves, or torturing themselves with everything from perfectionism to overthinking to having a crisis of confidence. These are the kind of misery-making habits of mind that kill our vitality (which I go into greater depth about in Gem 7 and Gem 9). But for now, let's step into our ability to be audacious and take the risks that will support us in manifesting our dreams. Audacity is one of the best antidotes to perfectionism I know. While perfectionism weighs us down, the brazen energy of Audacity inspires, enlightens, and lights us up!

Not only do you need your Audacity because it will take you far, but the world needs it as well. It makes no difference where you're at in your life, whether you're an aspiring, ambivalent, or out-and-out-parade-waving Audacious Girl (girl is a spirit, not an age), I say "Bring it on! Welcome and Amen, Sista!" It's our moxie, our spirit, and our feistiness that not only shines brightly in our lives but in the world around us. As we know, there are often risks and consequences when we own our more Audacious Self such as pushback from others, only you can assess which actions are worth it. When we allow the vitality of our spirit and our passions to guide our actions and behaviors, we automatically give others permission to do the same. As a result we all reap the benefits of a world with greater self-expression, freedom, and joie de vivre. How great is that!

> ✳ **LOIS-ism**
>
> **Practice Makes Progress.**

When we practice new ways of being in our lives and the world, we make tremendous progress. Here are some pivotal moments in both my clients', colleagues', and my own life that illustrate this. These are the top four reasons that I've found that show how expressing your Audacious Self opens up amazing possibilities.

Gold Nugget of Truth 1—Out with the Negating Nay-Sayers, in with the Positive Posse!

Several decades ago, I walked into a musical audition for a top children's theatre company. I was torn between performing my go-to safe, upbeat tune that usually gets smiles, and had already earned me jobs, verses a new song that was far more flamboyant. I looked at the two "bosses" sitting behind "the desk" waiting to say yea or nay to hiring me. One looked like his face was stuck in a perpetual frown (Mr. Perpetually Bad Day—P.B.D.) who made this strange sucking noise as if there was a piece of spinach terminally lodged between his front teeth that he was desperately trying to remove. The other, Mr. Crunchy Granola (C.G.), had a big shock of overgrown brown curly hair, a laid-back grin, and Birkenstocks.

I did what I call a "vibrancy check-in" which is about closing my eyes, taking a deep breathe, and tuning into my "little voice of instinct" in order to sense which song felt right to perform for that audition. The response was clearly biased toward going with the gutsier one, "I Hold Your Hand in Mine," a satiric tune by Tom Lehrer. It's a comedic number in which the character shares her love to her departed partner whom she has regretfully killed. Out of sentimental feelings, she keeps his hand with her at all times.

I gave it 1000%. Part way through the song, I pulled a rubber hand with a little trickle of fake blood from my bra and crooned to it. *Definitely* one of my more over-the-top numbers, because I sensed from the casting notice that energy, humor and moxie were the triple threat they were looking for. In general, I'm a "Go Big or Go Home" kinda gal.

Mr. Perpetual Bad Day started bellowing with his arms frantically flapping in the wind, "STOP! STOP RIGHT NOW!" like I'm a tractor-trailer with broken brakes barreling toward a busload of school children. The accompanist was embarrassed for me, and abruptly stopped playing and stared at the keyboard to avoid catching my eye.

At the same time, Mr. Crunchy Granola came running toward me with an entirely different reaction. His gestures were more of the Rocky-getting-to-the-top-of-the-stairs celebration variety. The two of them were a split-screen from different universes:

Mr. P.B.D.: "I've seen enough. In fact, I've seen *TOO MUCH*. Please leave."

Mr. C.G.: "Oh my God! I've been waiting for an actor like you all day. Passion, energy, and talent!"

I later found out that Mr. C.G. was piggybacking on Mr. P.B.D.'s casting call. Knowing that they had totally different sensibilities and were casting for vastly different companies it was unlikely that they would compete for the same talent, Mr. C.G. had first dibs on any of Mr. P.B.D.'s rejects. The irony is that I was both the top rejection for one company and the first choice for the other. When we go on the stage of our lives every day, we make ourselves crazy when we try to contort ourselves in order to please others. Many people are impossible to please, given who they are and who we are. However, we can learn to be true to our own authentic Audacious Selves, and play that role to the hilt! As Oscar Wilde said: "Be yourself, everyone else is already taken!"

I worked for Mr. C.G.'s company for the following five years. I traveled the country and got to perform for thousands of little ones who delighted in our innovative work. In contrast to what I might have experienced with Mr. P.B.D.'s company, I ended up having far more interesting projects, I was paid better, and clearly, was treated far better—because I was appreciated for who I was. During a break, I shared my other "safe" song with Mr. C.G. He smiled weakly and responded, "Nice song, but it didn't show your spunk. I'm not sure if I would've even called you back."

Same audition; two totally different reactions. For me, this is such a great reminder that by trusting in the moment and taking a risk, I found my tribe, and stopped taking rejection quite as seriously.

Gold Nugget of Truth 2—Audacity Builds Moxie

My client Cindy was feeling really bullied at her workplace. She's a contract consultant who was given absolutely no feedback on her work, even though she had constantly asked for directions and clarity about the client's or her boss' expectations. The company was in a hot mess and it was pretty clear her contract would not be renewed; most likely the company would fold. She had secured what is often called a "rabbi"—someone else on a lateral level with her boss, who respected her, recognized her skill and commitment, and offered to be a reference for future clients. All things told, she was in great shape, even though the company was not. Cindy, much to her dismay, heard that her boss was talking smack behind her back, basically saying her product was "crap" (he used some other choice words). Cindy was taking it hard and trashing herself.

In our session, I observed, "It sounds to me that you have absolutely nothing to lose and everything to gain by confronting him in an appropriate assertive (versus aggressive) matter." She looked at me like I had told her to put on a superhero costume and fight crime in her off-hours. She fought me on that suggestion, telling me that nothing good would come out of it and repeated all the terrible things her boss had said about her. "Exactly. The stakes are low. Clearly in dicey situations like this you need to take it on a case-by-case basis. But in this scenario I thought, what better time to flex your Audacious muscles in the gymnasium of life?"

It took a while, but she agreed. We did a strategy session, role-playing the best approach, language, and methods for staying present and eliminating any defensiveness. She practiced hard and came back to the next session absolutely on fire, ready to approach her boss.

At the next opportunity, Cindy walked up to her boss in a very calm way. She used one of my favorite key opening phrases, "I'm curious about...." when one's goal is to de-escalate a potential conflict but still approach the issue head on (more on this in Gem 11). When her boss responded, she asked what he meant when he referred to her product as "crap." As he writhed in discomfort, she saw the cowardly underbelly of this bully and was no longer intimidated by him. He finally cracked open and shared his discontent, which was vague and revealed his lack of vision and leadership. One by one, she addressed each point he brought up, not defending but addressing all of his complaints, her emails, and requested meetings asking for clearer directives in each area. He finally came clean about what a tough time the company was going through. He went on to admit that it was less about her (never coming clean that he threw her under the bus) but more about the restructuring/bankruptcy the company was dealing with. She thanked him for his honesty but added that she would have appreciated that direct approach right from the beginning. Inside, she was jumping for joy that she had succeeded at being her own advocate.

For the rest of her time there, he was on good behavior, and a tad nervous, around her. She also stopped hearing any gossip about her work. When things did fall apart, she left on good terms. Her boss genuinely thanked and acknowledged her for really hanging in there during rough times.

While audacity rarely accompanies universal popularity, it often brings integrity and invites respect. People know where you stand, whether they agree with you or not. In doing so, you're not only truer to yourself but you'll be attracting your tribe.

Gold Nugget of Truth 3—Your Passion Will Be Reignited!

Donna came to me as a smart, savvy, and somewhat burned out client. Her job had all the most deadening qualities: stressful, boring, and under-utilizing her talents. She felt guilty that she didn't have enough quality time with her son, but also felt exhausted and out-of-shape. Usually passionate about her life, she had no idea what she wanted to do next.

I asked her the question that always helps any stuck person access their Audacious Self: if she could do anything and she couldn't fail, what would the next chapter look like? Immediately, her eyes got wide and her seated posture became erect. Right away, she started talking enthusiastically about what she wanted to do next. Words flowed fast and furious like a dam had just broken. She wanted to start her own company, work only forty hours a week (vs. the current sixty), go to every one of her son's baseball games, and buy an unlimited yoga pass (and actually use it). I asked her how long she felt it would take; she said about eighteen months.

We did all the necessary strategic work, creating a plan, identifying the key members of her new business, upgrading her limiting belief systems, dealing with current crazy-makers in her life, and an assortment of other important actions. To our mutual delight, Donna accomplished her goals in twelve months, despite the unpredictable challenges along the way. When I asked her what part of our work together made the biggest difference, she answered, "Permission. You gave me permission to go for my dreams, and then I gave it to myself." At the core of the "permission" she referred, was the license to let her Audacious Self start doing the driving.

Audacious Role Models

I love making lists and having role models in my life, and these two naturally go together.

When I am going into uncharted territory, I find having a list of role models invaluable for two reasons. One, I'm able to tap into my imagination and think, "What would so-and-so do in this case?" In doing so, I come away with new ideas and a more expanded way of thinking. Two, it reminds me that many have gone before me, often in far grander way, with inspiring results. It also reassures me that it's okay to take my next audacious step. There are so many women in my life whom I respect and see their audacity. I highly suggest you create your own list.

To get you started, I've identified a few familiar ones who have the qualities that resonate for me, when I think of Audacious Women. They include:

* Mae West—Pioneer of women's free sexual expression, brazen, uncensored.
* Bette Midler—Outrageous, humorous, outspoken, bigger-than-life.
* Geneen Roth—Truth-teller, vulnerable, articulate.
* Gloria Steinem—Provocateur, pioneer of the women's movement, and visionary.
* Amy Schumer—Truth-teller, humorous, possesses lots of moxie, vulnerable.

* Anne Lamott—Outspoken, vulnerable, articulate, reflective, uncensored.

* Ruth Reichl—Vulnerable, adventurous, humorous, articulate.

* Kristine Zbornik—comedienne/singer/actress with lots of moxie, outrageous, hysterically funny.

I noticed these audacious women possess many of the following qualities:

* Visionaries.

* Pioneers.

* Full of moxie.

* Outrageous.

* Unconcerned about what people thought of them.

* Sometimes painfully transparent and vulnerable.

* Creative.

* Bigger than life.

* Fun.

* Humorous.

* Playful.

* Adventurous.

* Takes enormous risks.

* Enjoys financial and creative freedom.

* Transformative trailblazers.

By writing down the list, I got to identify what my version of Audacity looks like.

Yours will be different. Recently, I asked a few friends and colleagues who would be on their Audacious Role Model List based on what was most important to them. They shared examples of women who, while equally audacious as the women on my list, were less about being outspoken and outrageous, and more exuded the qualities of grace, equanimity, aesthetics, and persistence. Given that my friends feel more drawn to politics, architecture, beauty, and culture, those choices resonated more for them. We all have an individual imprint in terms of what audacity looks like based on values that are near and dear to our hearts along with what our interests are.

For example, maybe you're all about changing public policy. Your Audacious Girl's Guide talks about strategically setting up relationships with influential people in the political arena. There's no wrong or right, there's just what rings true for you!

So practice, my dear SPARKLE-Sistas. Practice being audacious every single day in small and big ways. When you do, you will get giddy, fall on that fabulous butt of yours, take it hard, laugh it off, and everything in between. I can promise you that by doing so, you'll feel that much more alive and many miracles will start showing up for you. I've seen it!

A Few Tips on Audacity

* **Make it your own.** My version of Audacity is not going to be yours.

* **Audacity is not a free pass to act badly.** It's about expressing your most authentic way of being, coming from confidence not defensiveness. It's making the choice to leave if that feels right, and is not the same as having no filters and rashly acting out.

* **Respect your cultural environment.** While it's important to be who you are, also respect the culture you're in

and tune into the outside environment as well as yourself. (Discussed further in Gem 8.)

* **Go at a pace that enlivens you but doesn't overwhelm you.** If you feel scared but excited, chances on you're right on that delicious edge of true Audacity.

* **Acknowledge yourself for doing whatever you do no matter what the outcome.** Speaking your truth will not always be easy, pleasant, or successful, but nothing can change the fact that it's *your* truth. Be prepared to get lots of "nays" and "yays." It's okay!

* **Look at the lesson** and make any modifications you may need to make it work for you.

* **Support others' efforts to be Audacious as well.** Offer your own experiences, lessons you've learned, and encouragement.

EXERCISE

✸   ✸   ✸   ✸

Exercise 1—My Audacious Girl's Role Model List

In your C2S Workbook, free-associate the first ten women who come to your mind. You can always add or subtract later. Once you've got your list, explore these questions:

* What is the common theme you see in their version of Audacity?

* Does that specific quality really feel necessary in you life right now?

* What is one small action you can take toward obtaining their unique Audacious Girl quality?

Exercise 2—Accountability Check-In

* Take one audacious action every day—small, like buying the more outrageous pair of glasses versus the same ol' same one; or big, like letting your point of view known whether people agree with you or not—and see how it feels in your body, in your energy, and your spirit.

* What is the self-talk that comes up around either taking those actions or having taken them?

* How do you feel afterwards?

* How can you support another SPARKLE Sista in her work at being Audacious?

Exercise 3—Discovering What Being Audacious Looks Like for You Right Now

In your C2S Workbook, list ten things you would be doing, feeling, saying, or planning if you were expressing your Audacious Self, right now.

* What has my Audacious Self been dying to say?
* To me?
* To others in my life?

Exercise 4—Being Audacious in Everyday Life

First, list three areas or issues in your life that you've been holding back in. Then explore the following questions.

* I'm holding back because:
* If I was willing to go for it, I'd do (and be) the following:
* Why those?
* How do I want to feel? What do I want to show up in my life as a result?
* What would be the best forms of support for what I need to do and how I want to feel?

Congratulations! You've taken the next step in your life! Celebrate! I can guarantee you that the more you put your Audacity Self out there, the more alive and aligned you will feel with your most authentic self. Your innate YOU-ness will come through, and opportunities will pop out of nowhere that you used to have to work super hard for. The clearer your path becomes, the more life will feel like a dance rather than a grind. Pay attention to what starts showing up as a result.

Check-In:

✳ What resonated for you in this Gem?

✳ What small or big action will you take?

✳ How will you get the support you need to do it?

GEM 4

✳ ✳ ✳ ✳

BRING YOUR DARKNESS INTO THE LIGHT

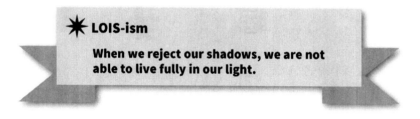

✳ LOIS-ism

When we reject our shadows, we are not able to live fully in our light.

I'm a hopeless optimist and a hopeful romantic. By being biased toward optimism, I stay curious and open. I have a resiliency that allows me to forge through the rough patches, appreciate my life, and keep on moving toward my dreams.

The irony is that even being a hopeless optimist, the pivotal moments that were game changers for me were when I was able to face my shadows and my fears. It was only when I was able to look at the aspects of myself that I rejected most vehemently, or expose my rough edges and process the feelings that came up, that I was fully able to celebrate my SPARKLE.

But even after all these years of self-work and optimism, when faced with uncomfortable feelings like anger, rage, sadness, and helplessness, I still find myself attempting to philosophize these emotions rather than allowing myself to feel them. I've seen over and over that experiencing our thoughts, behaviors, and actions is essential to living an authentic life of our own design rather than living from a place of default. I've also seen that, as the Buddhist's say, "understanding is the booby prize." Meaning, sometimes you just have to feel those uncomfortable feelings and take the uncomfortable actions in order to live a "Life that Lights You Up."

When faced with intense feelings often my fear is that I'll spiral down and never come up again, regardless that this has never been the case. I may rationalize that experiencing those feelings won't help me get through this rough patch, but in fact, holding them at bay actually prolongs the process of healing. As the saying goes, "What you resist, persists." Undealt with, our negative emotions will come up again and again to trip us up. I still may be walking the path to move forward in my life but it's like doing it with one leg hobbling.

Yet when I have the courage to sit with those feelings—not try to philosophize or catastrophize about them, but feel them—I find a magical thing happens: they pass. This is not in any way to dismiss the magnitude of certain feelings that we experience when dealing with the devastating pain of loss. Often, the grieving process has many layers of mourning. "Feeling the feelings" is a foundational aspect of healing but by no means in and of itself, is a magic elixir. I do find that having dealt with that level of loss in my life, the more I allow myself to feel those painful feelings, the more alive and more aligned I become. Things flow better in my life. I not only see it in my own life but with my clients and in my community. It takes courage, compassion, and curiosity to be with our shadows.

Even in the healthiest family dynamics, we all get messages pretty early on about what are "welcomed feelings" and what are "unwelcomed feelings," especially women. A woman cries. All of a sudden, it becomes a group project to get her some tissues to quickly "wipe away the tears," which I see as more wiping away the feelings.

Shame is toxic and eclipses our light. Yet when we ignore our shadows, we perpetuate the cycle of shame in our own lives and those around us. When we step into those forbidden feelings and befriend our shadow, we not only begin to heal from the cycle of shame, but fall back in love with ourselves and our lives.

There are many moments in one's life when acknowledging one's shadows prove transformative. These three moments stand out as an affirmation of why it's worth it.

Gold Nugget of Truth 1—You'll Have a Better Chance of Uncovering Your True Desires

One of the many reasons clients come to me is they "don't know that they don't know." Tara was a client who had told me that one of her top three goals was to have a meaningful, long-term relationship, but she had *no desire whatsoever* to get married. Her need to repeat it several times raised a giant red flag for further inquiry. After several sessions of hearing her out, I suggested she make a collage of her dream wedding. She rolled her eyes and accused me of not listening to her and was not happy with me. "Humor me. Do it anyway," I responded.

Despite great resistance, at the next session she brought in a beautiful collage, featuring gorgeous classic linen napkins, tasteful pastels and extravagant bouquets. I commended her for being a good sport, trusting the process, doing the exercise, and for her lavish vision. "It's just missing one very big element." She looked at me quizzically. "You!" I said. "Nothing in this collage represents your unique personality."

She turned back to her collage and said, "Oh my God, I have basically replicated my cousin's wedding!" As we talked further, my client realized that she felt like she had to measure up to her family's expectations by duplicating her cousin's epic wedding. Further complicating things, she really loved her cousin and considered her as a super put-together person.

After these epiphanies, I asked her what *her* wedding would look like. She got animated. She expressed enthusiasm for her alternative community, who gets together once a year, and what their traditions were. How she'd love an open-pit fire ritual, loud dancing, drumming and for her honorary sisters to collectively sew her wedding dress as part of the ritual. Tara lit up and got really excited, and in that moment, everything shifted for her. She declared, "I want to get married next year at our annual gathering." The timing was perfect. She was heading out there and was going to stay open to meeting a guy. She did *just that* and he would later become her husband. The following year, she was married in a wedding as unique as she was.

Had she not explored the shadows of her resistance, Tara never would have liberated herself from the unconscious picture of what her family-pleasing wedding *should* look like. As a result she was freed up to create a marriage that inspired versus restricted her.

When we allow ourselves to explore those fears and dark places, we not only learn more about ourselves but we gain clarity about our deepest desires. With this new-found clarity, we have a far greater chance of bringing those desires to fruition.

Gold Nugget 2—You'll Find Your True Voice

As far back as I can remember, I loved to sing. I'd do it everywhere: in the shower, on the street, everywhere. While I enjoyed it, I often felt this constant sense of frustration. No matter how hard I tried, no matter how much passion I felt, I only could make a pipsqueak, which was no match for what I thought must be my real voice. It was always a source of confusion for me since I have always had a very loud, contagious laugh and yet only this tiny singing voice would come out.

Fast forward to my nineteenth year, when I had just moved to New York City to pursue acting. Whenever I'd sing after doing my humorous monologue, people would always smile in a consoling way and say, "You do comedy, so you can get away with it." At that time, I was forty pounds heavier and lived on the top floor of a fifth-floor walk-up in Chelsea. I shared an apartment with an unemployed, yet wildly talented illustrator. We were both broke and neither of us could afford an air conditioner during that hot summer. So I was not only an aspiring actress but a perspiring one as well!

A friend of a friend referred me to Ron Raines, a veteran singer of opera, Broadway, and a roster of international performance arenas that would make most entertainers envious. When he was not on the road, which was pretty seldom, he worked with singers. I saved my pennies to meet with him, but I felt unworthy and scared. On the way to my lesson, I binged on chocolate cream-filled donuts. Sometimes the things we want the most in life are the things that scare us the most.

When he opened the door, Ron looked me dead in the eye and said in his thick southern drawl, "Darlin', let's get you over to the ivories." He motioned me toward the piano. He was 6'2", had a big, crushing handshake, and a deep Southern drawl.

I apologized for my small voice and he smiled in a "let's see about that" way and we ran the scales several times. Not only was I nervous but with the half-dozen cream donuts I'd eaten, I sounded more like a cappuccino machine brewing up a hot cup of joe instead of a singer. He passionately shook his head, "No." He stormed into the other room. "Oh, no," I thought. "He knows I binged."

He came back out and had a huge, thick belt and a fist full of cotton balls. I got an early jump on being a paranoid New Yorker. I couldn't help wondering if he was going to tie me up and put cotton in my mouth. I guess I'd been watching too many episodes of *Kojak*, the 1970s equivalent of *Law and Order, Special Victims Unit*. Instead of tying me up, Ron pulled his belt around my waist really tight and put the cotton in my ears so I couldn't hear my own voice. With one hand he made a fist and put it against my diaphragm, and with his other hand he ran scales on the piano.

"Darlin'," he said, "someone told you that you have a small, little voice and they were deeply mistaken. We're not here today to teach you to sing, we're here to help you find your real voice. The one that God gave you, not the one you think you have. It's like searching for gold; it's buried under mud and rocks. I can tell you, it's going to be BIG and raw and will probably sound UUUUGGGGGLLLLLLYYYYY. That's 'cause it's been buried for so long and is not trained. But you gotta let it be ugly before it can be beautiful. Is that something you're willing to do?"

I nodded in a confused way, but inside I felt like something was about to change. Ron instructed me that this time, all I needed to do was focus on pushing my diaphragm out so far that I'd "knock him clear across the room," pointing to his fist that rested on my diaphragm. We made a pact that as I went up and down the scales, I'd sing as loudly as I could, push out my diaphragm, and not listen to my voice.

With each set of scales, I gained a little more courage. Then something broke free in me and this huge, mammoth voice that was really ugly, came roaring out of me. It sounded like *Tyrannosaurus Rex* mating with a sea urchin in the next village. I was equally relieved and horrified: relieved to have broken through and horrified that this, indeed, was my *real* voice. I wondered if there was any chance I could get that sweet little pipsqueak voice back.

"Darlin'...did you hear that?" Ron smiled and gave me a high-five.

"Did I hear it? I think the customers at the 7-11 on the corner heard it!" I grimaced.

"Darlin', we found our first speck of gold. Remember we had to dig through all that mud and rock to find it. It's just a speck, but it's your speck and no one else's. There's a whole lot more mining, melting, and molding to do, but the first step is finding the gold, which we just did."

"Now, I don't always work this way," Ron went on, "but when I feel like someone's voice is trapped inside, I have to take dramatic measures for them to break free. You're very scrappy and a good sport. Thanks for being open to just jumping in."

In addition to Ron's fierce passion and commitment to uncover his students' authentic voices, he has a deep understanding of music, phrasing, and performance. That day, I needed to gain access to my true voice, not the one I was hiding behind. We hugged, I thanked him, and in a way, my life was never the same. He left on the road shortly thereafter and I wasn't ready to do the work anyway. But I finally understood why I was so hungry to sing, it was about the ability to express myself with the full depth of my passion and to uncover my real voice.

Ron put his finger on something I felt intuitively but had no words for; my true voice was trapped both literally and metaphorically. That pivotal moment started me on a trajectory of owning my voice on all levels.

When clients come to me, I help them to own their voice in many ways. Sometimes, it's gaining the courage to speak up for themselves when something doesn't feel right, and doing so from a place of clarity and worthiness. Other times, it's learning how to weave their accomplishments and skills into compelling stories so they can ace their interview and get the job. Whatever we do, it's ultimately about learning to trust ourselves and taking actions toward fulfilling their dreams.

No matter what the scope of the work that they do, and no matter how inspired they are by the goal, they will invariably have to face their shadows in order to accomplish their goals. In certain cases, just like my voice that was UGGGGGLLLLLYYYYY in the beginning, they must allow themselves to be imperfect, fall down, and do things poorly before they develop the necessary skills.

An example may be a client who is new to interviewing and has to go through the discomfort of putting herself out there. In the meantime, she stammers and blanks out until she becomes skilled at sharing how her skills will be an asset to a desired position. In another case, maybe someone made a mistake by speaking out of turn and needs to address the matter. It doesn't matter what it looks like but that they do it. When people are willing to move through the shadows in service of celebrating their light, they develop a tenacity, a deeper self-acceptance, and a gratitude that otherwise would never have been possible.

Now when I start my motivational presentations by singing one of my favorite songs, belting it out with my big voice and bigger-than-life spirit, people say, "Wow you have a powerful voice." I am reminded of the steps along the way to get there. I think of Ron, one of my earliest guides, who helped me own my voice.

Golden Nugget 3—Transparency Builds Intimacy

When I was five, my mother asked me, "What do you want to be when you grow up?" I responded, "Independent." My parents laughed hysterically, and shared it with many of their friends who also got a huge kick out of it. I loved the attention I got for being both precocious and "sharp."

But something else happened at the same time. I quietly started to construct my identity around being independent. I started working different jobs early in life, loved "doing my own thing," and being self-reliant. The downside was that I didn't face the shadow parts of self-righteous independence, which is about not asking for support, not relying on others, and not getting too close. When my life was spiraling downward and my parents offered to help me, I turned them down and merged my plummeting self-esteem with "independence." I found myself intolerant of and disgusted by people, especially women, who wanted to be taken care of; they were the lowest of the low to me.

A few decades later, I was taking a course on human behavior. I realized that I had conflated my desire for independence with an unconscious but grandiose conviction that if I didn't need anyone, I was somehow a more "together" person. When I dug a little deeper I found that—Yikes!—there was a part of me that would love to kick back and, yes, have someone take care of me. I was horrified.

After class I went back to Charlie's (my partner at the time) apartment, bereft. He was surprised because usually when I come out of these courses, I'm pumped up and restored to my usual hopeless optimism mode. Instead, I was very somber and revealed that I had a secret that I'd hidden all of my life, one that I was only now willing to look at. I let Charlie know the level of shame and embarrassment I felt about this new discovery. I asked him not to be judgmental, or negotiate me out of it, or slap on a smiley band-aid and tell me it's okay. "Let me sit with it, and if I cry, let me cry," I instructed him.

That made him super nervous. His gaze darted around the room, he started re-organizing the Ziploc bag collection, and offering me ten types of tea, which was wildly successful. I took a deep breath and shared my dirty little secret/shadow self: "While I'm independent by nature, I've been hiding out. There's a part of me that I've rejected all of my life, and that part of me totally wants to be taken care of."

I paused.

Stupefied, he waited for my punchline.

Giant pause.

"That's it? That's all?" he responded.

"Isn't that enough?" I said.

Charlie breathed a huge sigh of relief. "I assumed you were going to tell me that you have a life-threatening disease, are really a lesbian, on the run from the law, or breaking up with me—or all four."

We both burst out laughing. My big secret was no bigger deal than "pass the salt, please."

Charlie gave me a big hug and even teared up a little. He then confessed something I never knew. He shared how frustrating it was for him to want to take care of me and that my whole "independence shtick" actually made him feel less of a man. He also added how useless he felt at times when he saw how stressed out I was and was unable to help me, because I pushed him away.

Now I was the one tearing up.

Yet again, I saw the positive impact of embracing aspects of our personalities that we deem unacceptable, and as an act of courage, share them with those we love and trust.

After that conversation, I shifted from righteous independence to a softer, far more authentic interdependence. When I asked him for help, I feigned the damsel in distress role in a dramatic, "Honey, I'm just a frail, pale female—can you please help me open this jar?" over-the-top way. "I'm the man, let me open it, missy, that's my job," he responded, flexing as if he were a cartoon muscle-man.

Not only did I lessen my load a bit by asking for help, but his ability to make me happy gave Charlie an ego-boost that made him feel better about himself. When we embrace our shadows, we not only improve our relationship with ourselves but our relationship with our loved ones as well.

How to Begin to Acknowledge and Share Your Shadow Selves

I love this work because it frees up our emotional energy and allows us to really step into our lives in a whole new way. We do, however, have to do it in a way that feels safe and true to who we are and how we're wired. Here are some suggestions for doing that.

Start tracking your insights, either mentally or physically noting them. Start to notice when you go into fight/flight response. When you feel ashamed about possibly revealing something about yourself that you reject or might be rejected.

Breathe and let yourself experience the emotions that come up. This is probably the most confrontational step. When we swallow our feelings (literally and figuratively), we are re-absorbing them into our body. Rather than suppress them or judge ourselves for having them, we will be free if we can sit with them, breathe, and start to experience them as energy moving through your body.

The Top Ten Terrible List. Use your C2S Workbook and free associate the top ten dirty little secrets/shadow-self personality traits that you would be mortified to ever expose. If you feel shame writing them down, that's okay. It has to come out of you before you can work through it. Keep writing. You may surprise yourself; once you write them down, they may actually crack you up.

Shift from Criticism to Curiosity. As you go on with your day, when you find yourself judging your actions or thoughts, see how you can bring the spirit of curiosity to what you've learned. Ask yourself why you might feel this way, or what episode in your life might have taught you to hide this aspect of yourself. Understanding cause and effect can be freeing too, but don't let it override experiencing how it feels in your body.

Create a practice that will allow you to access your shadow self. I find that any kind of mindful practice that slows down our "monkey mind" will support us in that venture. It could be therapy, coaching, a support group, yoga, long walks, prayer, meditation, cycling, journaling, etc. Pick one(s) that speak(s) to you, not that you feel you "should" do. I have journaled since I was eight because it's something that always frees me up and gets me "current" with my emotional truth. Experiment to find the methods most effective for you. I go into greater detail in Gem 9.

Find a Creative Outlet. As I mention in Gem 7—Fire Your Perfectionist, my negative self-talk loosened its grip on me when I imagined my Inner Critic as an over-the-top character. As much as I loved my discovery in the privacy of my own home, I found it infinitely more rewarding to explore different aspects of myself in an enlivened and safe group setting. I started working with Elizabeth Browning many years ago, and to date, she is one of the most influential acting teachers and coaches in my life. She knows her craft impeccably and has a huge heart and she is brilliant at giving artists, even business people, a creative playground. She encourages her students to use sound and movement to explore all the different characters within themselves that, for many, were fraught with embarrassment and shame. To see people's faces light up and their true spirits come through from the freedom to express the full range of their emotions, creativity, and characters is transformative, both on a personal and professional level. Get creative, whether it's through acting, painting, writing or seeking like-minded people. Find a community that celebrates all aspects of yourself; not only your public persona.

Share your experiences with a loving and safe person in your life. Make sure to be very protective and only go to the people in your life who you believe can support you in this specific way. As I said earlier, if you don't have anyone in your life to share in this way, seek professional support. Match people's gifts and personalities with what you need at the time. If someone in your Sacred Circle loves to fix and provide solutions that may well be very effective when you're working on solving a problem. But chances are they may not be skilled at simply supporting you, and being transparent with them will be uncomfortable. You're not wrong and neither are they; it's not a fit. It's also okay if you're not ready to share with someone else, acknowledging to yourself that these parts exist and to give them a voice are a huge first step.

Be on the lookout for backlash. When we remove the shackles of shame by sharing and acknowledging our dark side, it's not unusual to have some backlash. There may be some feelings from your own growing edges or others who are attached to seeing you in an old way that doesn't serve you anymore. If your negative self-talk (or someone you consider a friend) starts screaming, "Oh my God—I can't believe you said that!" chances are you're in backlash territory. Fear not; it's the old way of being and being perceived that's shaking loose. Keep going, keep getting support. You'll get there!

Consistency is more important than intensity. Don't feel like you have to do it yesterday, but don't put it off until next year either. Do it now, but be respectful of how you navigate these waters. Don't overwhelm yourself. Go at a pace that grounds you, even if you have some negative reactions along the way.

Celebrate your Audaciousness. You're being fierce, true to yourself, and climbing back into your skin, your life. Congratulations! While at first you may feel "out of sorts," if you stay with the process you'll feel a genuine sense of relief, vitality, and greater energy from embracing your shadows. You are on your way to having the Courage to SPARKLE!

Support others' efforts to own their shadow. We teach what we need to learn. Nothing's more freeing than helping another dislodge themselves from the shackles of shame. When you hear someone else want to start sharing something that they're embarrassed about, check in and see if you're on firm ground in yourself. Make sure that you can be loving, and give them the "Bring it on!" message. Your relationship with them will never be the same and you'll have one more Audacious being in your life.

Doing is way more powerful than thinking. While it's tempting to "think about" or "read about" these exercises, you'll gain far more ground by actually going through the process and doing the exercises.

EXERCISES

✳ ✳ ✳ ✳

Exercise 1—Ballooning

When Ralph Kramden, the character Jackie Gleason played in the iconic sitcom *The Honeymooners*, got angry with his wife, Alice, and says, while shaking his fist, "Bang! Zoom! To the Moon, Alice!" we laugh. It was the exaggeration that allowed us to do that. If he looked at her seriously and said, "Watch yourself Alice or I'll hurt you," we would have, instead, gotten very worried and Ralph would have been the villain.

This same strategy of using exaggeration and our imagination, a technique I created called Ballooning, can be quite effective in defusing our worst fears. Have fun with this exercise; the more outrageous, the better. You'll know you're on to something when you stop taking yourself so seriously. It'll bring levity and lightness by addressing those fears with a sense of playfulness.

Example: Let's say you're a chronic people pleaser. While you may really like to help people out, there's a part of you that's really angry at having to say "yes" and then feeling resentful. You fear that under your "Terminally Nice Girl" there's a "*NO Woman*" lingering in the shadows. If you really let this exercise off the leash, you could visualize an over-the-top, anti-super hero sporting a fabulous outfit with the words, "NO, I said, NO!" emblazoned across her chest. Bursting into homes of the people she over-cares for and screaming, "Clean up your own life, damn it! Does the word 'NO' mean nothing to you?" Imagine the horror and outrage from her previously loving and caring circle. Imagine them triple-locking the door, banding together to rid the world of "NO Woman," ex-communicating her, and sending her to a far-off island where she'd be alone and not able to say "yes" or "no" for the rest of her life.

If that extreme reaction scenario sounds implausibly ridiculous, that's because it is! When we spin these elaborate worst-case scenarios in our lives, why not use the playful dimension of our creativity to break the cycle of shame and terminal earnestness and see what can open up for us? Perhaps, we'll discover that what we fear most won't happen and we're more resilient than we give ourselves credit for? Give it a go.

Pick the absolute worst fear that you'd be horrified to reveal to anyone and you most reject about yourself. Exaggerate the consequences of that discovery, and make it over-the-top until you can see the absurdity of it. If you are still under the shackles of shame, you haven't taken it far enough. Take it farther. Then answer the following:

* What did you discover by ballooning your dirty little secret/shadow self?

* What is one small action that you can take to start bringing that shadow into the light? It may look like being gentle with yourself and allowing that part to have a voice in your life.

Once you've done some work on your own, reach out to someone with whom you feel it is safe to share this. Be *very* selective with who you open up to. If you have no one in your life you feel safe enough to share it with (something to look at, too, if that's the case) think of working with a coach, or a therapist, or a well-organized, or safe support group.

Check-In

* What resonated for you in this Gem?
* What small or big action will you take?
* How will you get the support you need to do it?

GEM 5

✳   ✳   ✳   ✳

LIGHTEN UP WHILE YOU LEARN

I come from a long line of laughers. My dad would laugh so hard while watching Red Skelton (a very famous comedian/clown from the 1950s) on Sunday nights, his face would turn beet red, he'd stop making sounds, and his slight belly would jiggle up and down. As a little girl, I remember saying once, "Mom, is Dad having a heart attack or just laughing?" Of course, my mom laughed hysterically and said, "Just laughing, Lo!"

My mom, to date, is the only person I've ever met who relished being teased, impersonated, and satirized. It was pretty common during an elaborate party for her to hand my brother a dinner plate (to signify a steering wheel) and say, "Steve, do an impersonation of me getting on the highway," an activity that truly traumatized her. Clearly, she loved the attention and saw imitation as the highest form of flattery. She also knew intuitively that going public with something that really terrified her, laughing about it, and sharing it with others, would be both an elixir for her and help others to not take themselves so seriously.

My brother, sister, and I still share stories from our childhood that we find so funny that tears will stream down our faces. Thanks to my family, I got to experience firsthand the transformative power of humor and the ability to laugh at yourself. Whether it's a client or a difficult interaction with someone, when we make a choice to have a playful approach, it can not only de-escalate a challenging situation but allow us to bond with others and be more comfortable with ourselves. Humor and a spirit of playfulness when working on ourselves is essential, especially in those moments when our SPARKLE has gone south and we're on Dimmers. It's the quickest way to move to Shimmers.

As previously mentioned in Gem 4, I believe that we need to integrate both the dark and the light of our day-to-day experiences to be fully alive and genuine. I do find that the more we *choose* to lighten up about all this working on ourselves and meeting our goals, the more motivated we remain and the more we will enjoy the process. I see this with all of my clients and groups I speak to. There is enormous power in being playful in our quest to move forward in our lives.

Having a sense of humor is not even about being funny, memorizing jokes, or practicing comedic timing. After having done comedy for many years, I know that off-stage comics are some of the most macabre and forlorn folks I've ever met. The power to lighten up is an active choice to look at life through a very specific lens that sees the irony and frequent absurdity of life, and a willingness to both laugh at and learn from it. To do that though, you must commit to really *wanting* to lighten up, staying open to what shows up in your life, and shifting your perspective in the process. I can promise you that the more you look for the humor, the more opportunities life will bring for you to lighten up and stay more connected to your sense of vitality, your SPARKLE. Below are some ways to lighten up while you learn.

Look For and Laugh at the Irony in Your Life

I met a friend for dinner at a Thai place on the Upper West Side of Manhattan. The portions were microscopic and so were the napkins. After one too many spring rolls, which were delicious but greasy, we were in desperate need of a napkin. I'm always the Resident Big Mouth, who makes my requests known, albeit in a gracious way. However, my friend is really uncomfortable asking for even small things like this. I encouraged her to try her hand at asking. Since it was a low-risk scenario, it seemed like an ideal way to flex her muscles.

She reluctantly agreed that it would be "good for her" and asked for some napkins to wipe off our hands. The pint-sized waitress gave us each one cocktail napkin that didn't even clean one knuckle. Each time my friend asked for more napkins, the waitress handed both of us a single microscopic napkin. The irony of the fact that my friend kept needing to ask over and over and still got the same ridiculously small napkin was not lost on us, given the fact that it was so hard for her to ask in the first place. A total cosmic joke!

We literally couldn't stop laughing and tears streamed down our cheeks. The waitress came over to the table, and asked, "Napkin?" We nodded, incapable of speaking because we were laughing so hard. She bowed and handed us, yes, another ridiculously tiny cocktail napkin for our tears.

Clearly, there was a language barrier because we kept calling her over to the table till the manager came over. I explained to him that our hands were greasy and we needed *several* "big girl" napkins. Very politely, he said, "Certainly, Ma'am" and brought us an ample supply of normal-sized ones.

We both finally calmed down from our hysterical laughter, which so often arises when we get together because we love to laugh at ourselves and the situations that present themselves in life. One of the many gifts I get from this friendship. I asked my friend why she didn't ask for bigger napkins sooner. In almost every area of her life, she has excellent boundaries and communication skills (much of which I discuss in Gem 10). But when it comes to speaking up for herself in some very basic ways, she closes down. She shared a few stories about being yelled at when she was young simply for making mundane requests. She now saw how those experiences in her formative years left her emotionally shut down, even in making the simplest of requests. She smiled and said that the next time she felt reticent to say something, she would think of this situation. Reminding herself that no matter what happens, she would be okay and may even get a laugh out of it.

While finding the humor in our challenges doesn't heal us overnight, in time, it softens the pain and fosters a perspective of lightness.

How do you relate to this story? How can you apply it to lighten up in your life when different life lessons present themselves?

Spread Lightheartedness. It's the Only Thing Everyone Wants to Catch!

I have found that when I put my most playful aspect out there miracles show up in my life. While people are sometimes turned off and think I'm "too much," I almost always meet other tribe members who celebrate my SPARKLE.

One example was when I went to a very lovely but rather staid women's networking event that was sponsored by a retail company. I met some great small business owners and, while it was a "nice event," it was a touch low-key. I was in one of my punchier, more playful moods and there was this very sweet, shy woman in the corner. It turned out that her last name is Nightingale. Of course, I asked her if she was related to Florence, which she gets all the time, just like I get, "Lois...like Lois Lane and Superman." I figured it would be a way to bond on the cliché things people say at networking events.

I was in one of my more audacious moods so I started belting out one of my favorite Frank Sinatra hits, "If the nightingale can sing like you, / they'd sing much sweeter than they do." I lifted her hand, whereupon she got out of her chair and I twirled her around.

Everyone looked and started clapping. We both bowed. I sensed she really wanted to meet people but was too shy or intimidated. I figured since they were a nice group, if it fell flat, I'd take the hit and not her. Instead, the group was delighted and several people came over and complimented her. She was very introverted, so she was palpably relieved to not have to initiate breaking the ice.

Another lovely woman came over to me, and said, "You're supposed to be on TV, and I have a connection for you." What started out as a simple quirky act of playfulness in the moment, ended in the taping of five episodes on a local TV morning program with a local ABC Affiliate. It was a great venue where I shared my LOIS-isms and strategies for dealing with stress in a productive way. Not only was it great exposure, but it allowed me to really beef up my experience as an expert. It's amazing what shows up when we're willing to lead with our most playful, light-hearted self.

Use Laughing at Yourself as a Way to Bond with Others

When you laugh at your own imperfections and let others laugh at them as well, you create an instantaneous connection. Here are a few examples of how that has happened in my life.

A few years back, I created and facilitated a three-month program for the Navy on dealing with the stress of change. I worked with their civilian population and they were really terrific folks, who had to be very "buttoned up." Ironically, the decor of the room that we were in had a sculpture of a missile coming out of the ceiling. As I got to know them better, I joked around and shared the absurdity of working on our stress when weapons of mass destruction were literally coming at us. Obviously, I had to be careful not to be insulting but rather to bring a little levity to the training. A little titter of laughter followed my mention of the sculpture. That was a start.

While I toned down my own SPARKLE a bit, wearing slightly less dramatic clothes than I usually do to be appropriate for the culture in which I was presenting, (discussed in Gem 8) I still needed to be my authentic self. What I found was with each month they got more comfortable with me, and would comment about my SPARKLE. They'd say things like, "I was wondering what kind of bling-bling you'd be wearing this month." I found it deeply ironic that here I was, attempting to "tone myself down" so I could blend, and they were jazzed up by my more "bling-bling" attire. Once again, I found that when we express our most authentic selves, we give others permission to do the same. It's the lesson I keep learning over and over.

The real shift happened halfway through the training when the attendees were broken up in small groups to do a few exercises and activities. I took a moment to go outside to get some air and forgot to turn off my lapel microphone. I met a few people who were walking by and started to chat with them. Someone from my training seminar came out and in a very kind, apologetic way said, "Your microphone is on. We can hear everything you're saying." Luckily, I had only exchanged pleasantries. I thanked her and shut off the microphone.

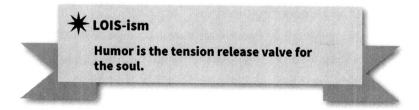

✳ LOIS-ism

Humor is the tension release valve for the soul.

When I returned after the break I said, "Thanks to Mary for giving me the heads-up since I was literally thirty seconds away from going to the ladies room and releasing some 'top secret' information that would've incriminated me." The whole room erupted with laughter. Laughing at my own giant faux pas had allowed me to bond with the attendees on a whole different level. They teased me for the rest of the training, asking me about "any top secret information" I was about to release. We had created an inside joke that I was happily the butt of, and the spirit for the rest of the program changed palpably. People felt free to share their foibles and challenges, and I experienced a level of appropriate transparency that really connected everyone.

I've given you a few examples from my experience of how humor has greatly impacted my life and shared some over-arching principles on the power of adopting a light-hearted perspective. Here's a few suggestions and guidelines for how to apply these gems on a regular basis.

Eight Whimsical Ways to Hit the Ground Laughing

Focus on being playful and lighthearted versus having to be funny. As I mentioned before, being playful is not putting pressure on yourself to be funny but rather to see the world and yourself through a light-hearted and playful lens. Don't feel you have to make a joke of everything but learn to see the jokes that are already there.

Use humor as a bridge versus a wedge. While the kind of sarcasm that puts others down (not the same as playful self-deprecating humor) can seem funny at times, as a regular practice, it drives a wedge between people. Humor that pokes fun at the situation and connects people in sharing a common absurd experience is far more healing and transformative for everyone involved. If you sense that you're about to say something snarky and biting that might get a laugh, I'd opt to not do it. You don't know how it will land on your audience, and the purpose is not to be funny or witty but to bring levity and light to a situation.

When you goof up or fall short of your own expectations, look for the humor. Nothing makes embarrassment or disappointment more bearable than seeing the irony or ridiculousness of your own situation. Look for it...it's almost always there!

Start small. If you fall into the terminally earnest category or you're going through a particular rough patch in your life, you don't need to put any undue pressure on yourself to immediately become amused either. Take a small action to bring a spirit of light-heartedness to your life. Big changes are created by small consistent actions.

Use common sense. If you have a high-powered interview and don't know the person who's meeting with you, don't pull out your "wild and crazy" Steve Martin self. You'll be uncomfortable and so will they. Don't bland yourself into oblivion either and hide your personality for fear of making a wrong move. Be sensitive to the environment around you and take it up a few (appropriate) notches.

Create low-risk situations for yourself to practice a spirit of light-heartedness. When I was a stand-up comic, even now when I'm testing out a new story or comedy bit, I'll do a "drive-by beta test." For example, I may find a way to weave a story into an interaction at my local bank or bring my levity to the grocery line. If it flops, who cares? I'll never see these people again, I don't have to care what they think.

You're not a project that needs to be fixed, you're a person who's evolving. When we're working on ourselves and our goals, looking at what stops us, it's easy to start treating ourselves like a damn fixer-upper! I've done that and so has almost everyone I work with in one way or another. Like a gem that SPARKLES, we have many facets and some jagged edges. Depending upon how the light hits us or the situation we're dealing with, it's common to feel disappointed by the dull spots in our lives or feel broken and need a total overhaul. Life is messy; change is even messier. One of my favorite songs, "Masterpiece" by Jessie J, shares how she messes up sometimes and that she's still "working on my masterpiece" that is her life. What a glorious message to share with the world! Your life is a masterpiece and each day you are working on it. The more you celebrate the process, not the product, the less you'll feel like a project.

Take humor breaks. I have a colleague who was going through a very gray period. While she's by nature a positive person, between some significant personal and professional challenges, she was in a bad way. Being proactive, she took all the pretty standard and recommended actions (medical supervision, exercise, diet). One thing she did every day when she got home from work was to watch about thirty minutes of silly animal videos on YouTube and laughed the whole time. She reported back what an amazing effect that had on her spirit and her energy.

Decades of research proves that it boosts your endorphins, serotonin, feel-good hormones, and positively impacts your immune system. Plus, it's just plain fun.

EXERCISES

✳   ✳   ✳   ✳

Exercise 1—Laugh while You Learn

Here are some writing exercises to explore in your C2S Workbook. Don't over-think it. Usually the response that comes up first is the most spot-on.

* List three things that you're willing to laugh at yourself about.

* List three things you're willing to lighten up and allow others to laugh at you about.

* List three things that you are not willing to laugh at yourself about or allow others to.

* Given what you've learned in this Gem, list three ways you can laugh while you learn.

* Ask yourself, when I mess up or fall short of my goal a few new ways to look at it are:

* Select a specific challenge happening in your life. Then pick your favorite sitcom (e.g., *Modern Family, Frasier,* or *Seinfeld*) select your favorite character, and ask yourself the following questions:

  * If *X* was dealing with my challenge, how would s/he address it?

  * How would they make fun of it and bring some levity to it?

  * How can I do the same?

Check-In

* ✳ What resonated for you in this Gem?

* ✳ How will you apply it?

* ✳ What small step can you take right away?

GEM 6

✳ ✳ ✳ ✳

ILLUMINATING YOUR UNIQUE WIRING

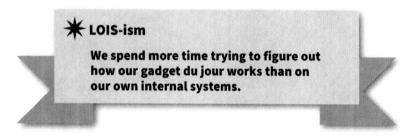

✳ LOIS-ism

We spend more time trying to figure out how our gadget du jour works than on our own internal systems.

We all come with a hard-wiring system. It influences our social interactions, our emotional life, the way we process information and outside stimuli, and the natural pacing of our activities. Life tinkers with the hardwiring (as we can ourselves), but we often spend more time figuring out how to use our Smart Phone (or in my case my Outsmart Phone) than how our own system works. Understanding and working with our wiring is a key element toward experiencing a greater sense of empowerment in our lives. When we take the time to examine that system, and the experiences that modify it, we can then access what I call our Owner's Manual. There are many components that make up our Owner's Manual. In this Gem, we'll be focusing on the emotional, mental, and social.

Emotional—Knowing Your Default Emotional Wiring

Computers, iPads, and iPhones have a default setting based on their wiring and so do we. I call ours Default Emotional Wiring (DEW). These are set-points that show up in our lives under duress or subconsciously, as our automatic responses, reactions, and behaviors.

A classic example of one of these set-points is when we naturally feel the need to go to sleep, what hours of the day we do our best work, and when we naturally wake up without an alarm clock. We have those same default settings in our emotions as well, both non-productive and productive. Starting to really observe what our DEWs are and how they serve and undermine us, can be exceedingly helpful in understand our innate wiring. There's no right or wrong, even with positive or negative emotions, but rather those that bring about non-productive versus productive results.

My DEW on a non-productive level is despair and feeling overwhelmed. When I'm exhausted or things aren't going my way, I can easily backslide into either or both states. If I don't address those feelings, I experience what I call a malaise like low-grade fever: not sick enough to be bedridden but not well enough to be on my "A" game. I find it ironic that a motivational speaker deals with low-grade despair, hopelessness, and being overwhelmed as their emotional default setting! Clearly, we all teach what we need to learn.

My most productive DEW is curiosity. No matter what's going on in my emotional life, I'll always look for ways I can use what I'm going through to learn, grow, and help others to do the same. It is through my wiring to be curious that I identified this concept of Default Emotional Wiring. I see DEW in all my clients as well as people in general.

The more skilled we become at understanding how our gadgets work, the more versatility and benefits we can derive from them. I believe it's the same as when we have greater access to our Owner's Manual. It's deeply rewarding for me to see my clients' circuitry light up when they finally understand why they're doing what they're doing. Better yet, find new ways to implement more productive behavior. It provides so much more freedom for them and allows them to move from as I've mentioned, Criticism to Curiosity. What was once viewed as "What's wrong with me?" is now viewed as "How am I wired with regards to this issue?"

> ✳ **LOIS-ism**
>
> **Our greatest assets can be our greatest liabilities, but our greatest liabilities can become our greatest assets.**

It's so exciting to discover that the brain is an evolving superhighway of neural transmitters. Just as we can build new roadways and tributaries to take a more direct route to our physical destination, so are we able to do the same with our thought processes.

Even *seemingly* negative emotions can serve us sometimes. Someone can say how terribly stubborn they are and see how it really undermines them. Yet, stubbornness is a key component in tenacity and persistence. It's all in how you use it. When we move from criticism to curiosity and become aware of how we're wired, we have a better chance of leveraging emotions that rarely serve us to serving us and others. The first step, however, is becoming aware!

Why It's Worth the Work to Discover Your DEW

I've always known that I'm an exceedingly sensitive and empathic person, I didn't realize to what extent. Several years back, I took my mom for an outpatient procedure. Even though she was being properly treated, as they started their work, she winced in pain. My heart broke. I gave her my hand to hold. As soon as she held my hand, the pain that she was experiencing literally ripped through my body from the top of my head to my toes; a lightning bolt of agony. As soon as the procedure was over, I asked her how she was doing. I knew what she would say, so when she responded, "Lo, it was crazy. The second I held your hand all the pain went away," my own lightbulb went off. I had heard the term *empath*, when you literally experience others' pain, but I had no idea that I was one.

More and more, I saw that my non-productive DEW of despair and being overwhelmed was not only about my own feelings. But that I was also picking up those feelings from those around me and sometimes the world at large. Now, so many more things made sense: my inability to see violent movies or watch the news for more than a certain amount of time or the amount of stimuli I can handle without getting overloaded.

Being sensitive gets a bad rap, as though you're fragile but that's not true. You need to mindfully navigate life. In my case, that includes monitoring my level of stimuli, making sure to engage in mindfulness/refueling practices (meditation, journaling, creative work, and rest) on a consistent basis, really addressing issues directly as they pop up, and avoiding potentially toxic people and situations.

I get flack for my sensitivity on occasion. Ironically, it is often the same people who love my sensitivity when it serves them. My ability to empathize when they're having a rough day, or intuitively pick up when something feels off that they need to look at. But when it's inconvenient for them and ruffles their feathers, I get pushback.

While it used to really bother me, I've come to terms with it. There will always be people who criticize us for how we're wired. While it can hurt our feelings, it's important to hear what they have to say, integrate what can help you grow, and leave the rest behind. In addition, we have to be adaptive to others' styles as well. I truly believe that when we honor our innate wiring on all levels, our natural resilience and true spirit is able to shine through. Ironically, the more I respect and honor my sensitivity, the more resilient and thick-skinned I become. We must honor our DEW. It allows us to grow and develop in a way that is organic to who we are and to shine brightly in the world.

Mental—Identifying and Honoring Your Natural Pacing

One of my favorite children's fables is *The Tortoise and the Hare*. The Tortoise and the Hare are competing in a race. The Hare can sprint much faster than the Tortoise and starts off way ahead. Then, prematurely cocky about his win, he naps under a shady tree. Only he wakes up and discovers he's the loser. The Tortoise, though plodding, kept a consistent, slow and steady pace and became the winner.

We are in a different kind of race, becoming busier and busier with more obligations and choices for how to spend our time, none of which is going to slow down anytime soon. When we feel stressed out and struggle with "time famine"—the experience that we're running out of time—we don't always make the best choices. It's easy to feel like we're terminally busy but not very productive. Often by operating that way, we can either delude ourselves that we're accomplishing more than we have, or we just burn ourselves out—either way, not reaching the goal.

I find the folks who excel at realizing their goals are NOT always the fastest ones or even the most naturally talented. But what they *are* is very clear about their goals, good time managers, and keenly aware of their skills and challenges. Most of all, they are working in accordance with their natural pacing.

Defining Your Natural Pacing on the Tortoise and Hare Scale

Inspired by this classic story, here are the four most common archetypes I've used to help my clients identify their own pacing:

HARRIED HARE

These are the Type-A folks. They live adrenaline-filled lives and intermittently have crash-and-burn cycles. These crashes require lots of time, energy, and money to reboot them and "catch them up" after spiraling down. They say that's how they thrive, but I am quite dubious about the truth of that assertion because I see the impact this lifestyle has on them. Often, this frenzied pace comes with poor decisions, non-existent self-care, and a wake-up call that often consists of a health, financial, or dramatic crisis. This is the profile of someone literally addicted to their own adrenaline.

MINDFUL HARE

Then I know people who do absolutely *thrive* on adrenaline-based pacing yet are very successful and maintain a healthy lifestyle. They do their best work when they have multiple projects going and thrive with a fair amount of intensity.

My dear friend Nancy is one of those people. She is a brilliant massage therapist, business owner, yoga instructor, and organic herb aficionado. It's typical for Nancy to be running a thriving massage therapy practice, training the therapists while doing many sessions herself. In her "down time," she is usually taking yoga classes, overseeing a renovation on a family property, growing her own herbs, cooking her own meals, meditating, reading three books at once, and several days a week, cycling fifteen miles a day. "Another day, another interest to pursue" is Nancy's motto.

From hearing about her busy lifestyle, you'd think she'd be a Whirling Dervish who is on her way to burnout. You'd be wrong. While Nancy is a caring person and a great friend, she also knows she's a solitary type person who needs tons of alone time. She really understands her wiring and paces herself accordingly, valuing the power of refueling and is impeccable with her self-care. She gets eight hours of sleep a night, no matter what, and follows a diet optimal for her in a totally non-neurotic way.

I recently sent her this passage to make sure I had accurately characterized her. Within an hour of sending it to her, she wrote back, "You're right. I'm a Mindful Hare with *shpilkes*—ants in the pants."

I laughed out loud because I neglected to mention, along with her other "downtime" activities, she's teaching herself Yiddish. She's not even Jewish! Nancy does a lot but she breathes a lot, too. She is the epitome of a Mindful Hare.

CLASSIC TORTOISE

Years ago, while I was training to be a coach, I had the opportunity to work with this amazing woman as a practice client. We'll call her Franny; a quiet, demure, and very shy person. She would apologize for how slowly she spoke, the small deliberate ways she tended to her life in academia, and how much of an outcast she often felt. Her kids, well-meaning, would sometimes make fun of her "turtle-like" slowness in her approach to her life. She said she had tried to speed up. But the more she did it, the more she would boomerang into an almost inertia-like state.

I asked her about her life, personally and professionally, and I was slack-jawed at the depth of her accomplishments. She came to this country at the age of ten without speaking any English, got her PhD as an adult, became one of the top academics in her field, heading up her department, and created ground-breaking systems for alternative learning models.

I asked her why she thought she needed to change, as she was clearly being harangued by her internal Itty Bitty Committee, a term I use for negative self-talk. She was far more successful than those "Harried Hares" she was around, yet she still felt pressured to conform. She teared up and blurted out, "It's like I'm a turtle or something." I asked her what was wrong with turtles. I reminded her that they live a long life and are incredibly resilient. In certain environments, they can speed right along though in others, they must slow down. With their incredibly developed defenses, they are highly adaptive, adding to their strong survival instincts. They're not pushovers, they know how to bite.

She laughed and told me that she lives in a rural town outside of New York City, where a wild turtle literally crawls into her backyard on a regular basis. She thought it was odd but never gave it much thought. I told her it was her Animal Mentor there to give her a message.

I suggested Franny name her and she came up with Tilly the Turtle. When Tilly visited, Franny would look at her through the kitchen window and ask her what the lesson was today. What Franny noticed is while other creatures would pop in and pop out, Tilly would slowly, step-by-step walk from one side of her property to another in a careful, intentional way. She grew to love Tilly, who reminded her of herself. Slow and steady in both her personal and professional life, and she did "win the race."

Everything Franny does is slow-paced, intentional, well-thought-out, and well-executed. She takes her time, she rarely makes costly or time-intensive mistakes. That's been her secret sauce all the time. The difference is that now she no longer tries to be someone she's not and has embraced her pacing. Franny is a Classic Tortoise.

THE TURBO TORTOISE—STEP-BY-STEP IN FITS AND STARTS

Then there's what I am: the Turbo Tortoise! I work best with a combination of careful step-by-step planning with a few fire-under-my-butt lifelines (I don't like the word deadlines, it creates unnecessary anxiety) to keep me energized and engaged in the process. But a steady stream of this kind of schedule overwhelms me. I've come to understand the power of that scrappy little mechanism in the brain called the amygdala that triggers the fight/flight reaction when danger is approaching. It was essential to our survival during cave days to avoid the charging mammoth. It's still helpful now, obviously, but doesn't always know the difference between genuinely life-threatening emergencies and that work lifeline. That's why slowing things down and taking goals step-by-step allows me to go under the radar of the amygdala. It re-engages my pre-frontal cortex, where creativity, critical thinking, and goal-setting take place.

Given my preferred Classic Tortoise model, and the lightning-fast way my mind processes ideas, thoughts, and connections, I need intermittent fires under my butt to keep me engaged. These intense bursts of energy and focus fueled by an ambitious deadline, allow me to bypass my attraction to distraction and give my overactive imagination a playground in which to channel my ideas.

If I only went with the Classic Tortoise model, I'd be uninspired and feel bored. With my DEW of being overwhelmed, if I only maintained a Harried Hare rhythm I'd get distracted and stressed. I'd feel like I'm running a race with sandbags attached to each hip, frantically trying to "catch up," and pursuing that "fake finish line." Neither extreme is productive, fun, or sustainable for me. But together with a clear project date and specific deliverable in front of me, I'm grooving. That's me, the Turbo Tortoise! When I crash and burn or get stuck, I know I need to return to the step-by-step part of the Turbo Tortoise.

What Instrument are You in the Orchestra of Life?

Once I was working with my massage client named Bruce, who has cerebral palsy. He's fierce, kind, and an eternal optimist despite his physical challenges. A friend had purchased the massage as a gift for him to receive some healing touch and address some of his chronic physical pain. Bruce's life story is a fascinating one. As he shared his journey while I worked on him, his body frequently moved erratically followed by short staccato movements, none of which he had control over.

Each time the spasms happened he'd say, "Sorry, sorry." I could feel the shame wash over him. While I kept assuring him that it was totally okay, his self-consciousness was affecting his ability to relax and let the massage do its magic. As I continued to work with him, I began to see the movements of his body as different jazz artists improvisationally riffing through his muscles.

Bruce being a jazz aficionado, I shared this metaphor with him. "Hey, Bruce, let's guess which jazz artist's work your body is playing."

Bruce let out a big laugh and softened a bit. As his leg swirled around the table from one side to another followed by a rapid-fire beat with his hand, he exclaimed, "Damn, that's Coltrane if I ever heard him!" Now, I smiled. His hands then began moving in a smoother, more rhythmic motion he identified as Etta James. As I worked deeper into his muscle tissue, he started to have rapid, electric-like sensations throughout his body that he called his "Inner Scat Singer."

"Hey, Bruce, does your body take requests?"

Bruce smiled and shook his head, saying, "No way, it plays whatever it damn well pleases!"

What started out as a source of shame and tension became a playful game of "guess the jazz artist." We started to joke around and had so much fun. He got some deep healing in, but mostly I felt it was an opportunity to see his body through a different lens. By the end of the session, Bruce was visibly more relaxed and I had learned something very valuable. When we get creative instead of being critical, we start to relax and can shift our perspective in a more productive way.

Several years later, I spoke to a community of artists and I remembered my session with Bruce. Using a somewhat similar analogy, I asked them, "What Instrument are you in the Orchestra of Life?" A woman who had been very quiet in the seminar, smiled and said, "Violin." She shared that even though people thought her very fragile, she was quite resilient. Like the violin, she saw herself operating in life in a precise way that has made her a leader, much like the violin carries the melody for the orchestra. Then a man bellowed, "I'm the tuba, everyone knows when I'm in the room." The momentum picked up and everyone started piping up with the instrument they identified with most. Then they started guessing each other's instruments—accurately.

What I loved about this exercise was how it quickly connected the group while also sending an important message that there was no right or wrong when it comes to how we're wired emotionally. A cello is no better or worse than an oboe, it simply sounds different and needs to be played differently. It's the same when considering our own instrument and how we can play it to enhance its best qualities in the orchestra of life.

Each instrument contributes in a different way to make an orchestra's sound richer and more multi-layered. Applying the metaphor to myself, I realized I'm the soprano sax, high-pitched but soulful, and can easily cut to the core of the emotion of any jazz number.

I can't help but see the parallel with life. With the complexity of group dynamics, it's pretty common to try to blend in by pretending to be someone we're not. Yet imagine if we use a quarter of that time, energy, and focus on learning how to best use our own instrument in the orchestra of life. What if we started to figure out how to play our own instrument more skillfully and in a meaningful way? What if we looked at the challenges from a place of curiosity and patience when the "orchestra" is a tad dissonant and off-key? Imagine the beautiful music we could create living our own life as a result!

Different Pacing at Different Times

I've had a few Mindful Hare clients who felt particularly raw after a setback and needed to do a therapeutic Classic Tortoise for a while. But once they regained their footing, they returned to their natural pacing. Similarly, you may have certain areas of your life in which your pacing looks very different than others. While you may have certain proclivities when it comes to your rhythms and pacing, certain life lessons are harder than others to master, and sometimes, your pacing may change accordingly. You may say this is "common sense," but I'm here to say that for the most part it is "Common Sense—Uncommonly Practiced."

When Time is Scarce

A client of mine who is a Mindful Hare by nature came to me slammed with a beyond-full-time job, a daughter struggling with college applications, a deep commitment to her self-care, and maintaining her forty-five-pound weight loss. She was also eager to develop an idea she had into a book or novella.

I suggested she work on her book fifteen minutes a day, three days a week. She knitted her brows, but did it anyway. Nine months later she had 240 pages. The impact of this strategy appeared when her company unexpectedly laid her off. She already had a body of work that reminded her how much she loved to write and edit versus what she had been doing. She was so excited to try her hand at freelancing and she's never looked back.

Addressing Pacing when Dealing with Emotionally Charged Goals

A colleague of mine was haunted by her unfinished dissertation that was quickly approaching its expiration date. She had a lot of conflicting responsibilities, all of which were important to her, but she was plagued by this *incompletion* in her life. Every time she walked past her home office and saw her stack of research materials, she was reminded of her "failure." Time was running out, but her life was as busy as before, on top of which she had deep feelings of regret and embarrassment.

She had a year left to complete her dissertation, and even though it was against her "type," she shifted from Mindful Hare to Classic Tortoise. She committed to fifteen-minute sessions every day with rewards before and after, a concept I call "reward sandwiches" which is about incentivizing one's self to do a difficult task by scheduling in a reward before and after.

When she shared her idea with several colleagues, they offered tepid, polite eye-rolls of "good luck, but that doesn't seem realistic" reaction. She was committed to completing it in a way that felt rewarding to her. A year later, she received her doctorate. That's the power of honoring your resistance as well as deliberately working with pacing.

Honoring Your Capacity

Mental and emotional bandwidth is the amount of mental and emotional energy and focus required to fulfill a task, project, or goal. For most people that I see struggling with feeling disconnected from their SPARKLE, it is more often about not being realistic about the amount of mental and emotional bandwidth their lives require at this point. In this case, rather than thinking in terms of bad or good choices, I'd strongly suggest you look at what is or isn't working for you. If whatever you're doing is working, great. If not, it's time to make some changes. On the following pages are a variety of tools to support you in building a life that holds meaning for you.

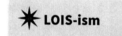

✳ LOIS-ism

Capacity = Time + Mental and Emotional Bandwidth.

Powerfully Choose

So many of our thoughts, actions, and behaviors are unconscious, which is both to our advantage and our disadvantage. Imagine if you had to remind yourself to blink, breathe, or walk; you'd never get anything else done! There are a whole lot of unconscious behaviors and beliefs that dictate our actions and impact our lives as in a way that does and doesn't serve us well. The more conscious we become of the motivations of our actions and emotions, the more we can choose which ones will actually benefit us.

I'm a huge fan of the term "powerfully choosing." We make choices all the time, often by default. Not choosing is a choice in and of itself. That's why it's essential to choose either to do something or not.

For example, I always knew I'd go back for my undergraduate degree. I wasn't sure when but I knew I would, and because of that I was at peace. I was powerfully choosing not to go back yet. Granted, I was busy with other goals, and at times, definitely rationalized that it wasn't the right timing. For the most part, I didn't torture myself about it. Once I did powerfully choose to go back to school, I knew I would accomplish it. There was a vitality in my path because of it. We must have a healthy understanding of and willingness to be honest about our decisions to take something on in order to move toward our goals and dreams. When my clients turn down a suggestion I give, after having considered their emotional and mental bandwidth along with what's on their plate, I applaud them because they're powerfully choosing not to do it, rather than avoiding it. Sometimes, they may change the time line or the size of the task and at other times they need to ditch it altogether. In doing so, they are learning to honor their emotional bandwidth so they can be freed up to powerfully choose what they most want to use their time energy and resources to accomplish.

Honor Your Mental Bandwidth in Each of Your Goals

Let's look at the sample goal of starting your own business as a piano teacher. You're someone who's always had a staff position. While you're excited, you're also clueless about how to begin besides printing up business cards. You're uncomfortable going to networking events, not sure how to price your services, or where your clients hang out for purposes of advertising.

You can *still* do it, but it's best if you factor in the mental bandwidth piece of it. I'd assess that the mental bandwidth that is required for this business would be fairly high due to the unknowns involved in developing a private practice, such as licensing, accounting, taxes, and the general learning curve of any new venture. You need to consider that while moving forward and building your business.

Bring in Your Pacing Archetype

Only you can decide the best approach, but consider your Pacing Archetype. The following are simply suggestions to help you get started.

Classic Tortoise—Take micro-actions in every area and celebrate each one.

Turbo Tortoise—Focus on only one or two areas for a short period of time. Schedule some intense work sessions to make some sizable progress. Scale back to a more moderate pace to keep the momentum going without overwhelming yourself.

Mindful Hare—Pick three or four activities, go full force for a longer duration, but build in tons of self-care and down time. In your "spare time," take a few actions in the secondary focus.

Harried Hare—Do the same process as the Mindful Hare, but be honest about admitting that if you don't put in some self-care you will crash and burn. Consider carefully if you're willing to pay the price of "rebooting." No one can live exclusively on caffeine!

Social—Honoring Your Social Wiring

Marianne Williamson, a pioneer in the spiritual movement, shared this touching story of how her daughter learned to connect in new social situations. Her daughter was about four years old at the time and relatively outgoing in familiar social settings. However, when meeting strangers for the first time, she was cautious and would wrap her arms around Marianne's leg, while scanning the room. Once settled into her own skin, she found new people who interested her, and then would simply let go of Marianne's leg and join the group.

Marianne shared that her daughter wasn't looking for any reassurance or any soothing gesture from her. She simply needed to feel her mother's presence and take her time before integrating herself into the group in a way that felt natural and right for her. Initially, her daughter needed a fair amount of time before inserting herself into new social situations. But by honoring her own wiring, very soon she only needed a few minutes before disengaging from Marianne's leg and joining the group. Marianne gave her daughter the gift of a safe haven. In doing so, she sent her a powerful message, "You know your way, trust it." That sense of permission will take her far.

We can all learn a great deal from this example about navigating our own social process as well as supporting those we love in doing the same. That story has deeply influenced me. I'm very social and outgoing by nature. Yet when I throw myself into social situations without thinking about how I need to enter them, I find myself either trying too hard or not being able to develop an authentic rapport. When I follow my own version of what Marianne's daughter knew so instinctively, taking my time to find my own bearings first, before "seeking my tribe" in the room, and then joining in, I have a terrific time. When we connect with ourselves first, we automatically connect with others on a more rewarding level.

Closing the Gap between Knowing and Doing when Honoring Your Wiring

We've covered a lot of territory in this Gem, from the many aspects of your Owner's Manual to best approaches on how to move forward. Congratulations for doing the work! For some of you, this type of work may be a great reminder and reinforcement of what you know to be true for yourselves. For others, it may be a whole new way of thinking. Most importantly, it's about implementing what you know. More than any one question, I'm often asked, "I know what to do and yet I don't do it. What do I do about that?" I call this Closing the Gap between Knowing and Doing. Portia Nelson's piece illustrates this beautifully.

AUTOBIOGRAPHY IN FIVE SHORT CHAPTERS*
by Portia Nelson

CHAPTER ONE

I walk down the street.

There is a deep hole in the sidewalk.

I fall in. I am lost... I am helpless.

It isn't my fault.

It takes forever to find a way out.

CHAPTER TWO

I walk down the same street.

There is a deep hole in the sidewalk.

I pretend I don't see it.

I fall in again.

I can't believe I am in this same place.

But it isn't my fault.

It still takes a long time to get out.

CHAPTER THREE

I walk down the same street.

There is a deep hole in the sidewalk.

I see it is there.

I still fall in...it's a habit but

my eyes are open.

I know where I am.

It is my fault.

I get out immediately.

CHAPTER FOUR

I walk down the same street.

There is a deep hole in the sidewalk.

I walk around it.

CHAPTER FIVE

I walk down another street.*

Take time to discover your Owner's Manual. You will "walk down another street." When you do, you will experience the Courage to SPARKLE.

✳ LOIS-ism

Practice Makes Progress.

This is a LOIS-ism worth repeating. Please be patient yet persistent with yourself while you're in this process. When you find yourself falling short of honoring what you know is right for you, whether it's an old pattern that keeps repeating itself, or a recent faux pas, let this be your mantra. Here are some ways to practice what you've learned in this Gem. Go back to your C2S Workbook, and go through these exercises.

*Reprinted with the permission of Beyond Words/Atria, a division of Simon & Schuster, Inc. from THERE'S A HOLE IN MY SIDEWALK: THE ROMANCE OF SELF-DISCOVERY by Portia Nelson. Copyright © 1993 by Portia Nelson. All rights reserved.

EXERCISES

✴ ✴ ✴ ✴

Exercise 1—Getting Curious about Your Pacing

✳ Which of the four Pacing Archetypes (e.g., Classic Tortoise, Turbo Tortoise, Mindful Hare, or Harried Hare) do you relate to?

✳ Why (e.g., Classic Tortoise: I am more effective when I take things step-by-step)?

✳ How does it serve you (e.g., I'm less likely to make costly mistakes)?

✳ How does it not serve you (e.g., sometimes my slow pace is due to feeling like I need to have every single detail in place. If I just focused on the top priorities I may be more efficient and meet others' expectation in a more timely manner while having more downtime for myself)?

✳ How would you like to adjust it to work better for you in your life (e.g., get clarification on top priorities while keeping others in the loop)?

✳ What small action can you make (e.g., map out the key steps of the project along with timeline and send to my team so they can rest assured I'll get the project done)?

✳ What support would be helpful (e.g., make a suggestion that we all do that so everyone understands and respects how each of us like to work)? Remember, letting yourself off the hook and accepting "Hey, this way works best for me," is a small but mighty action.

✱ The biggest takeaway from this section is...?

Both identifying and honoring your personal pacing is imperative to Creating a Life that Lights You Up for the following reasons:

✱ Ability to trust yourself more.

✱ Greater compassion and awareness of your innate wiring.

✱ Ability to move forward with your goals and dreams in a logistical and emotional way that makes most sense for you.

Exercise 2—You are Your Own Role Model

Identify one to two goals you've accomplished in your life in a successful (your definition) way. An example may be that you were able to sustain your accomplishment and didn't get sick or hurt yourself in your process of getting there.

✱ What did you do to make them happen (e.g., accountability, structure)?

✱ How can you apply that to your current goal (e.g., get support)?

✱ How can you get support to honor your innate pacing? (e.g., buddy call)?

Congratulations! YOU are your own role model!

Exercise 3—Assess Your Bandwidth Emotionally and Mentally

Make a list of all the things you're dealing with in your life, right now. They don't have to be goals, but they can be. Here are some examples:

* Learning how to communicate better with my new boss.

* Getting our finances in better shape.

* Being more active and losing weight.

That's only part of the list for some. Most of us have many more. They may or may not be life goals but rather a combination of aspirations you want to achieve as well as fires you're putting out in your life. But you still need to assess the energy and effort they're going to take.

Exercise 4—Reflection Question: What Instrument Are You?

* What instrument are you in the orchestra of life (e.g., soprano sax)?

* Why do you relate to that instrument (e.g., it connects me to the core of my emotions)?

* What are three qualities of that instrument resonate for you (e.g., soulful, intense, high-pitched at times)?

Knowing your instrument, what are three ways you can play it more effectively on a daily basis (e.g., monitor my stimuli, focus on what touches my heart and spirit, recognize but not apologize for my intensity)?

How will you use that to make beautiful music in your own life (e.g., know that the people I gravitate toward are intense, sensitive, and highly creative in their own way; very sensitive and equally resilient; and celebrate that and laugh about it... often)?

Exercise 5—Identifying your Default Emotional Wiring

* Check in with yourself three to five times a day for the next week and notice what you're feeling.

* Where do you go emotionally almost automatically on a daily basis?

* Write it down.

* Start to identify both your productive and non-productive DEW.

* Put them in a list side by side and start narrowing them down to one or two in each category.

* Be patient but persistent, since most of us are on automatic pilot a lot of the time.

* What are your non-productive and productive DEWs?

* How does your non-productive DEW stop you? Be specific.

* How does your productive DEW support you? Be specific.

* What actions can you take with your non-productive DEW?

* How can you best leverage your productive DEW?

Check-In

* What resonated for you in this Gem?

* How will you apply it?

* What small step can you take right away?

GEM 7

✳ ✳ ✳ ✳

FIRE YOUR PERFECTIONIST

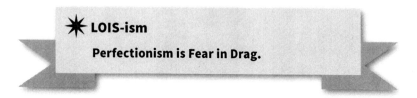

✳ **LOIS-ism**

Perfectionism is Fear in Drag.

I was a event at Barnard College—an all-female liberal arts college in New York City that is part of Columbia University. Barnard is considered one of the most influential colleges, especially when it comes to cultivating female empowerment and feminism. I met Debora Spar, the president of the college. She is smart, accomplished, and very accessible. I'm passionate about and familiar with the contents of her terrific book, *Wonder Women; Sex, Power and the Quest for Perfection.* Spar's book chronicles not only the history of the feminist movement, but looks at the metrics of women's ability to break the glass ceiling in many male-dominated professions. While she clearly highlights how far women have come in many ways, it's revealing to consider the myriad of fields where the number of women in leadership roles still hasn't risen much. Spar also addresses how women are still plagued with perfectionism.

I see perfectionism as a contributing factor to what stops women from breaking through what I call Shattering our Inner Glass Ceiling. I approached President Spar and we chatted about how prevalent perfectionism is and what a huge role it plays in stopping women from going after what they want. Spar underscored her thesis: that even when women aim ambitiously high, and even when they achieve their powerful goals, many still often have that "not good enough" feeling. As she was sharing her experience of the issues at hand, I offered a mischievous grin. President Spar looked at me in a quizzical manner.

"I have a LOIS-ism for perfectionism. Wanna hear it?"

She nodded yes, slightly amused yet curious.

"My LOIS-ism is, 'Perfectionism is Fear in Drag!'"

She laughed out loud. "Oh that's great—and so true."

We chatted more about the impact of perfectionism that she sees not only in her students but with her very accomplished daughter as well. It's clear that President Spar is deeply passionate and committed to not only spreading awareness of this issue, but implementing some solutions. She's a delightful woman. As I was leaving the venue, I heard her share my LOIS-ism with her other colleagues and they laughed as well. Hopefully, it went viral within the Barnard walls, but more importantly, drove my point home.

I see perfectionism as the silent thief. It steals our dreams, our vitality, and often our self-esteem. The overall sense of fulfillment that one would hope would accompany success often fades in the shadows of perfectionism. It is insidious as well as overt in its attacks. But when deconstructing perfectionism down to its core element, it is fear—plain and simple. What keeps a person stuck in the vicious cycle of perfectionism is often a deeply complex and unexamined, underlying belief that we are not good enough, and therefore, nothing we ever do is good enough.

Perfectionism usually surfaces in two extremes. One scenario is what I call "I'll never be perfect so why bother," in which we make NO attempt toward a specific goal. We make this ridiculous demand of ourselves to be perfect and are unwilling to go through the uncomfortable, messy process of learning. This mode of perfectionism leaves us feeling stuck and immobilized. By the way, this is the largest deterrent to even starting something. Want to set up permanent residence next to a blank page? Tell yourself you're going to write the next Great American Novel.

The second form of perfectionism is being relentless in trying to reach an unrealistic ideal we've created for ourselves, often bludgeoning ourselves in the process. It's not because the standard is too high, but rather that the driving force is a belief of not being good enough. I liken perfectionism to eating a delicious healthy meal, yet being unable to digest it fully. Instead of being properly nourishing, it just sits in our stomach and we're left feeling bloated and exhausted.

I often get pushback from hardcore perfectionists when I bring up how detrimental it is. "What's wrong with wanting to be the best you can be in all areas of your life?" My response is that it's a fantastic goal. But I call that *mastery*, which is not the same as perfectionism.

Mastery takes similar relentlessness and rigor to achieve. To me, that sacred place is where the human and Divine meet. To spend hours, weeks, months, and even years on a project that holds meaning for you and to get it to a level of precision in service of your own standards, brings about a certain satisfaction; that's mastery. It's awe-inspiring and terrific. When I speak about perfectionism, I'm not referring to a person's desire for mastery.

So what is the difference between perfectionism that is damaging versus attempting to achieve mastery in something that holds meaning for you?

The difference between mastery and perfectionism is rooted in our motive. Mastery is motivated by our passion for excellence that drives us to work on something, often relentlessly. You will invariably fall on your butt and course-correct along the way. You'll experience a divine restlessness when you fall short. There is however, a sense of exhilaration. The journey to mastery is rooted in a deep desire for excellence and there's a tremendous feeling of worthiness and fulfillment even if at certain moments we are frustrated.

Perfectionism has a very different motivation. Perfectionism is often fueled by a deep wound of feeling not good enough. As a result, one creates an unreasonable and often amorphous ideal, a mythical bar to hit that is not rooted in reality. The motive comes from a desperate need to fix a part of us that feels broken, flawed, or is craving a sense of approval. It ultimately has nothing to do with the tasks at hand. It is housed within a fantasy that when we arrive in this mythical *perfect* place, then we will *finally feel good about ourselves* and heal our old wounds of not feeling good enough. But that won't happen. It can't and it never will. The emotional hamster wheel of perfectionism only leads to a contraction of our true self.

At this point you may be saying, "Hmmm... okay, I get the difference between the healthy pursuit of excellence and the unhealthy obsession with perfectionism, but what do I do about it? How do I tear down the wall of perfectionism that on a daily, weekly, or monthly basis stops me from believing in my own value?"

When dealing with core wounds and messaging from childhood, depending upon the level of severity or trauma that one has experienced, therapy and therapeutic modalities can be very effective. I often suggest them to clients and they have achieved successful outcomes. The techniques and principles that I am suggesting here are both a wonderful complement to the deep work of therapy as well as being very effective as stand-alones to loosen the shackles of perfectionism that most women suffer from.

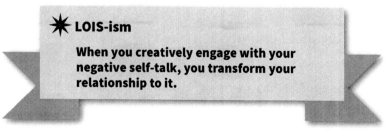

✷ LOIS-ism

When you creatively engage with your negative self-talk, you transform your relationship to it.

Get to Know Your Inner Critic

Inside every stuck person who suffers with perfectionism, there's an Inner Critic that hasn't been explored, identified, and re-purposed. But once we do all three, magic happens. We claim that part of us that's scared, and we gain access to that energized part of us that "wants to do it anyway." Creativity is the bridge that joins both aspects of us together. Here's how that happened for me.

On a miserable rainy day, I was in my apartment attempting to work on my stand-up comedy routine. Training to be a stand-up comic is a difficult job that we often have to do in the least inviting environments. The training grounds for testing your material are often a host of open-mic nights in dive bars, with the occasional worn-out billiard table, and uncomfortable metal seats filled with depressed comics and a few drunks hovering over the bar. Charming!

That day, the environment in my apartment was worse than all the miserable open mics I'd ever gone to. I had to stare down my worst enemy—my Inner Critic (IC) and that day my IC was in full voice. While I have a whole cast of characters in my head that both taunt me and celebrate me, I focused on my Perfectionist, aka IC. I see my entire Itty Bitty Committee—the scrappy crew of negative self-talk characters who clamor endlessly in my head—as neighbors in the same mental condo complex; separate units, but they share the same wall. You may open a dialogue with one, but the others get the message, too. My Itty Bitty Committee was particularly relentless that day.

I was stuck, resigned, and in pain. Nothing's worse than a belly full of desire and a head full of negative self-talk. Nothing I could do was right, and everything I practiced *sucked*. Or so my IC told me.

I'm both blessed with, and sometimes challenged by, a mind that churns constantly. For the most part, I get a daily delivery of what I refer to as *divine downloads*. They consist of ideas, concepts, stories, life lessons, acronyms, and alliterations being pelted at me non-stop—often before nine am. While I'm grateful for how creatively my mind works, the challenge has and probably always will be the "Big Shiny Object Syndrome." I become smitten with the new sparkly idea or concept, get distracted, jump around, and lose focus. This is something I see all the time with highly creative and entrepreneurial folks who can get easily distracted. Yay! I'm a triple threat!

However, that day I was in such deep despair, feeling so beaten up by my nasty IC that I became numb and collapsed on my couch. I was about to turn on the TV and watch anything, just to shut out those voices. All of a sudden the idea came to me: "I wonder what my IC even looks like? Is it man, woman, or creature? What is its name? What does it wear? Most importantly, does it accessorize?" I became intrigued.

I know from comedy that while every idea must come from a kernel of truth, you have to exaggerate it a bit to extract the humor and shift your perspective. There's no better way to do that than to recruit the rich world of your imagination. I started imagining my IC/Perfectionist as this character named Helga: part Viking, part army drill sergeant, part dominatrix. She has oversized combat boots, a ridiculous, too-big Viking helmet with horns and fur. She wears a breastplate made of E-Z Foil aluminum pie dishes over a jacket with oversized shoulder pads from the 1980s, and a whip that's made of a dirty mop. She's a cultural mutt, with a part-German, part-Nordic, mostly-Monty-Python-esque accent. Her mantra is "You vill do it perfectly or you vill do it not at all!" She then bangs her mop down and hits her toe in the process. I started laughing and walking around my apartment holding a mop pretending to be Helga. With each rehearsal, I made her more clownish and ridiculous.

My relationship with my negative self-talk was never the same. Not that it doesn't chronically visit me; it does. The difference is that when it does come up now, I try to isolate the individual characters that are expressing themselves. I imagine what they look and sound like. I create a healthy distance from them, utilizing the tools of creativity, compassion, and comedy to address the wounds that used to take me out for days, weeks, months, and even years. With tenacity and a whole dose of patience, I ultimately pry loose some of the criticism by having more than a fair share of visits with Helga.

That single practice of really identifying and bringing Helga out of the shadows brought miraculous results. I worked with her very consistently and started to break from the shackles of perfectionism. From having chronic stage fright, relentless writer's block, and self-criticism to a year later writing and performing my one-woman show called "Tea with the Demons." It was a show about making peace with our negative self-talk by turning them into over-the-top cartoon characters. I also wrote three more shows, performed stand-up, and became an arts educator, sometimes performing for groups as large as 1,500. It certainly didn't happen overnight, and while it wasn't the only work I did to address my perfectionism, it made a key shift in breaking open my resistance.

When I do this exercise with my clients and with my groups, they first need time to get past the initial "You want us to do what?" reaction. But they invariably have fun creating their own Itty Bitty Committee, especially the Perfectionist/Critic. By far, this is the most widely identified member of the committee. If attendees are still feeling the sting of their critics, I urge them to make their committee members even more ridiculous so they can have a sense of humor about themselves.

The characters that my clients have come up with are of sheer brilliance: the Hermes Mom carrying the $350 diaper bag; the Deranged Parochial Schoolmarm with a pitchfork; the E-Trade Baby having a temper tantrum; Thigh Woman, who is comprised of two 1,000-pound thighs stuck together; and the Whirling Dervish of Crapdom, a mythic character that swirls with disco lights in a tornado-like movement. While it's fun to come up with different characters in your imagination to help you lighten up and give you perspective when it comes to dealing with your negative self-talk, ultimately it's about implementing the exercise in a way that resonates for you.

One example is a client who was writing a book to share his expertise, attract more business, build his brand, and to be of service to his clients. While he's very talented and a great writer with a wonderful sense of humor, he was being stopped by his Itty Bitty Committee. During a coaching session, he shared that he was constantly barraged by his Inner Critic. The negative voices would yell at him that he was doing it wrong. "Sometimes, it's so loud I can't even hear myself think," he reported. We talked about what his IC looked like and then created a practice that would help take away some of its power.

We came up with a plan for my client to start a daily writing session with the same empty chair next to him that we would call his Inner Critic/Inner Editor. Whenever he found himself derailed by his negative self-talk, he would look over at his chair and say, "We're writing, not editing. When we get to editing I'll enlist you, but for now, I'm going back to my writing." Once he did that, the resistance (often at the core of the IC) calmed down and he was able to stay in writing mode. He not only completed the book, but he received rave reviews for it and positive feedback about how much value it provides for his clients.

For my client, the ritual of bringing the chair over to his desk was a practical and powerful strategy in acknowledging his Inner Critic while at the same time not giving it so much power. While we spent a bit of time exploring what his IC looked like, his ritual helped to signal the beginning and the end of each writing session. Doing that was his way of giving voice to the IC while reinforcing his own ability to take charge.

One of my female clients wanted to start a coaching business but was always judging whether she was "good enough." Her IC, Hermes Mom with the $350 diaper bag and perfectly coiffed hair who *had it all together all the time,* became a regular part of our coaching work. When my client was confronted with taking on a big action, I'd ask her to close her eyes, connect with her IC and ask what she had to say. What first started as yapping "You'll never do it," and "Unless you're perfect, it won't count," eventually brought up deep feelings of fear and sadness. We were then able to identify core beliefs that were stopping her and worked diligently to shift them. By doing so, she was able to move beyond them and take the necessary actions to build a thriving business that inspired her and helped lots of women.

When we give voice to our IC and become creative with what they look like, make them cartoon-like, we lighten up our perspective and are less likely to be so controlled and manipulated by them. I've done this exercise many times, and what amazes me the most is the energy that gets freed up. We create these wonderful characters in our imaginations which keep us entertained and engaged for hours. As adults, we have the power to leverage our creativity and to loosen the grip of perfectionism and move forward toward our dreams.

SUGGESTIONS

Connect with your IC before doing something that scares you. The more you give voice to that part and see the absurdity, the more you'll connect with your most vibrant self and the part of you that wants to do it anyway.

Pace yourself. If this is new and confronting for you, simply do it for five minutes so you don't overwhelm yourself. Your capacity will grow.

Learn how you learn. How do you learn best? Are you visual (seeing), auditory (hearing), or kinesthetic (feeling)? Use whatever is your natural method of learning to do this work. If you're visual, you may want to collage or draw these characters. If you're kinesthetic as I am, you may need to put on music and move. If you're auditory, both music and talking out loud may be the way to go. There's no wrong or right way, there's only the right way for you!

Try journaling/dialogue work. Many of my clients find it invaluable. You may choose to dialogue with your IC and then write back as that part of you that is committed to moving forward on a project. It's okay to argue on the page with your IC if that's what comes up. See how you can create an open dialogue with both your IC and the part of you that is really excited about moving forward.

Make peace with your Inner Critic. The more you do this work, the more you'll find your IC is not as bad as you think. As you strip away the layers and stay in dialogue, you may discover that your IC is really not that ominous, but is only hiding behind its loud bravado. I liken the process of getting to know our IC with that wonderful, revealing moment in *The Wizard of Oz* as

Toto pulls away the curtain. We see that the Great Oz is merely a tiny little man perched on a stool pulling levers in an attempt to project an omnipotent image. The more we get curious versus critical of that part of us, the more freed up we'll become.

REFLECTION

* ✳ What does your Inner Critic/Perfectionist look like?
* ✳ How will you powerfully choose to have some healthy distance from it?
* ✳ How can you find a way to have a sense of humor about it?
* ✳ How will you use it on a practical level to let the Itty Bitty Committee know who's in charge?

Evidence List

When we face new opportunities that both delight and scare us, it's essential to remind ourselves that we are way more competent, confident, and resourceful than we realize. Here's where creating what I call an "Evidence List" is really helpful.

One of my favorite definitions of fear is "False Evidence Appearing Real" (not a LOIS-ism). So much of what we fear is based on what happened decades ago and may have no relevance in our current reality even though we keep bringing it up. An Evidence List is a great opportunity to reinforce and remind you of your myriad of talents, gifts, and accomplishment—basically, who you really are.

Here's a sample Evidence List for someone who needs to reinforce how resourceful they truly are: (i.e., a great way to support yourself when dealing with taking on a new project where you're not sure how to proceed).

1. I spearheaded a local food drive while having a young child by simply staying focused, doing one thing at a time, and asking for help.

2. I'm very skilled at asking the right people for very specific advice when dealing with a situation I'm not experienced in. Most people almost always feel a sense of satisfaction knowing they were of service.

3. With almost everything I've created in my life, I had no idea how it would happen. But the more I committed to it, and shared my excitement with others, the more I enjoyed the process and allowed others to join in.

4. Once I establish my top priorities, I'm a natural researcher, critical thinker, and can usually map out the process to get there.

5. There are so many free resources out there that if I do some asking around and research, I can probably find what I'm looking for.

You get the picture!

SUGGESTIONS

Write the list. Now. Don't wait until you're feeling totally stuck to write the list since you probably won't be at your best and be able to see your natural gifts and talents.

Read it regularly. I'd suggest reading your Evidence List on a regular basis, three to five times a week, especially in the beginning. Of course, if you're having a tough time, take it out, and read it. The more you can make it a regular part of your practice, the better. Grab a moment when you're on line or in traffic and grab a peek.

Write it down in your own handwriting. When you write the list longhand, you'll access a different region in your brain that will evoke a far deeper emotional charge. Reading a list in your handwriting is ultimately far more potent than a typewritten list, which can look impersonal.

Start with one list. You can have multiple Evidence Lists, depending upon the particular challenges and ways you'd like to leverage your resourcefulness, but it's best to start with one at a time.

List both personal and professional accomplishments. Both are equally important.

Keep it simple. Make sure not to have more than eight or ten items listed; five to six is preferable. If you write too many, you'll start to ignore all of them.

Keep it handy. Fold up your list and carry it in your wallet so it's easy to find.

Be present. Read it out loud and really luxuriate in each of those items listed. Think of each one as a delicious piece of chocolate. You want to take your time really enjoying each luscious morsel.

A client of mine found this Evidence List very helpful when transitioning from a long-standing staff position to venturing out on her own and reconnecting with her love of travel. When she felt panicked about her goal, she'd breathe, read the list, and look at all the previous changes she had successfully made in her life. She calmed down and was able to reconnect with her love of adventure and travel.

Good Enough is Great!

Another way to fire your Inner Perfectionist is to firmly establish your version of Good Enough. The concept of *Good Enough* has been around for a long time, but it's usually given a bad rap. It's often synonymous with settling, or even being a slacker and getting by, but I actually think it's the complete opposite.

As a recovering hard-core perfectionist, the concept of *Good Enough* has been an invaluable tool for me. I have found it to be very useful for me when I'm up against my perfectionism in the classroom of life. I was first introduced to the practical application of Good Enough about five years ago, and it has stayed with me ever since.

For most people, dealing with change, even those that they have worked very hard to achieve, is still very confronting for them. Change upsets the old paradigm and brings about a fair amount of anxiety in the process.

Dr. Sara Denning is a clinical psychologist by whom I was certified to integrate her Adaptive Behavioral Health model into my work with individuals and groups. Dr. Denning's Adaptive Behavior Model focuses on three key areas; the biology, biography, and behavior of addressing chronic anxiety. Biology identifies one's own individual wiring; biography, the role one's upbringing has had on anxiety; behavior, how one presents themselves in the world as a result.

A key element of Dr. Denning's work that I address with my clients is for them to establish their own version of "Good Enough." By engaging in this inquiry and establishing their own criteria, they are far more capable of meeting their goals in a way that is meaningful to them while loosening the grip of perfectionism. I've witnessed the power of Good Enough in my own life as well.

In 2013, and for the following two years, I was spearheading my mom's care, with my brother and sister, while she was in hospice. Before my mom entered hospice, she was in and out of hospitals for at least a decade. Her health issues were not only a huge challenge for her but put a considerable strain on myself as well as my two siblings.

My sister Lori, a very active member of Team Edie (Mom), saw me sweating it from time to time because I had forgotten to ask the doctor a small question that wasn't vital to Mom's care. Lori saw me beating myself up for the oversight. She turned to me one day and said, "Lois, never forget, it's a marathon not a sprint." Conversely my sister, who has five children and a packed schedule, would feel badly on occasions when she wasn't able to visit Mom with the same frequency that she usually did. I'd remind her as well, "Lori, remember, it's a marathon not a sprint."

As a family unit, my brother, sister, and I, were all deeply committed to providing Mom with the Rolls Royce of care, given her limited mobility and pretty severe health issues. "It's a marathon, not a sprint," became the mantra that sustained us to stay on track with Mom's care, while being compassionate with ourselves along the way. "It's a marathon, not a sprint," was our family's version of Good Enough, and it was really useful.

I share that exact phrase, "Good Enough," with clients who are dealing with long-standing issues with either difficult people, situations, or projects that have many moving parts. Being given permission to not have to be *perfect*—whatever that means—calms us down.

The Science behind Good Enough

I've written in previous Gems about the fight/flight mechanism deeply rooted in the part of the brain called the amygdala. When we are in the throes of perfectionism, we are stopped dead in our tracks and the amygdala has a field day with our nervous system. How many of us have sat down to do something that was both important but confrontational only to find ourselves glazing over and wanting to surf the net as a distraction?

When we adopt the principle of our own Good Enough, we can loosen the grip of having to be perfect and we can make some small but consistent changes in our lives. We can give ourselves the gift of celebrating our progress and acknowledge, "Wow, I've come a long way, baby." Day by day, when we commit to our own version of Good Enough, we have a far better chance of getting there.

I strongly suggest you try on the concept of Good Enough.

Developing Your Good Enough Strategy

Let's say your daughter dawdles in the morning before school and it drives you crazy. Right now, you're either having a power struggle with her where she knows she has something over you and you're losing it, or you've totally given up and feel resigned. You're trapped in a pattern. Your perfectionist might tell you that, "A good mother doesn't lose it, no matter how stressed out you are," or "You didn't say 'let's get going' in the nicest way."

Think of your reaction on a continuum. Where are you versus where you'd like to be? Maybe your ideal version is the ability to be totally non-reactive, bright, and cheery. Nice on paper but given your time constraint and your lack of sleep, it is most likely not a possibility for you, right now. Your Good Enough may look like taking a few deep breaths and reminding yourself that being warm and fuzzy isn't feasible. Staying calm and focusing on the task at hand will have to be Good Enough. From there, you can ask yourself what action can help get you where you want to be.

By taking the pressure off yourself, you will find your re-sourcefulness. For example you may decide to wake your daughter up twenty minutes earlier and you being totally prepared on your end will give you greater wiggle room if she drags her heels. Or, you may discover that mornings are not your best time. Perhaps you can swap getting your daughter ready with your partner and take on one of the evening chores when you have more mental bandwidth.

While many of the solutions you come up with may be based on common sense, when you're triggered, you're not always in the place to implement them. Adopting a Good Enough approach begins to create a sense of resourcefulness to do that.

Suggestions

Go through the entire process. The first few times, I'd suggest you go through the exercise at the end of the Gem, write it down, and review your responses. After a while, you can go through the steps mentally and you'll start to experience what Good Enough means and a true sense of relief with it.

Move from Criticism to Curiosity. You'll notice this LOIS-ism a lot in this book. That's no accident. As women, we can be relentlessly critical with ourselves and the more you move from criticism to curiosity, the more you'll be able to shift and actually enjoy the process of moving forward. As you're trying on new ways of thinking and behaving, you will fall short of your goals and have setbacks. Look at a child who's learning how to walk; they stumble into cabinets, take a few steps, and then fall. Consistent encouragement and course correction (which is discussed in greater detail in Gem 12) allows you to make the shift.

What Good Enough isn't. To reiterate, when I say "Good Enough," I'm not suggesting you label behavior that doesn't serve you, or is plain acting out, as Good Enough. I'm talking about being both compassionate and honest with yourself while supporting yourself in a way that works for you.

Do a Good Enough Check-In. When faced with the tyranny of perfectionism, stop, breathe, and ask yourself, "What would Good Enough look like for me, right now?"

EXERCISES

✳ ✳ ✳ ✳

Exercise 1—Naming Your Inner Critic

Close your eyes. Take several deep breaths and imagine what your Inner Critic (IC) looks like. If you're a body person like me, you may need to move around a bit or put on music that will help you connect with your IC. If so, keep your eyes at half-mast so that you don't bump into anything. I can assure you that your Itty Bitty Committee will have something to say like, "This is stupid, you should be working." If so, you're on the right track. It simply means you're breaking down your resistance, and your resistance is feeling threatened. Keep going.

Think of the cruelest thing you ever say to yourself. That is where the core of your IC lives. At first, you may feel really triggered and stopped by it, but keep going. Imagine your IC saying that mean thing, but add an element of absurdity—maybe an accent, baby talk, or gibberish. The bigger and more absurd your IC becomes, the more you'll be able to gain a lighthearted perspective of it. Keep going. Once you get the image, give it a name. Don't overthink it. My Helga IC used to be named Magda—it doesn't matter. The first one is usually the most visceral, so go with it.

Now, see how ridiculous you can make this character look in your imagination. Embellish the character with accessories to make it a more fleshed-out experience. Exaggerate your IC character with huge gestures. When you start to smile or see how absurd the character is, you've hit gold. Explore, play, and have fun.

Open your eyes and congratulate yourself! It takes courage and moxie to really look at that part of you that's been operating in the shadows for so long. Life is precious, your dreams and goals are even more valuable. Don't let your IC be the deciding factor as to whether you live a fulfilled life or not!

Afterwards—really rest! When you start loosening the grip of resistance and giving a voice to your IC, there is often some backlash afterward. Make sure to prepare for it. You may experience a barrage of the Itty Bitty Committee's "This is so stupid. You've been duped." Whatever. This is where journaling is really helpful, or doing something nurturing for yourself, like taking a bath, is essential.

Exercise 2—Evidence List

* Select the top goal or issue you're looking to address in your life. Start with one thing and feel free to repeat using additional ones. (e.g., you want to take your business to the next level: what does that mean?).

* Identify the specific challenges and fears you have (e.g., I am not very good at technology, and I'm overwhelmed by how I will be able to handle many aspects of it).

* Name themes and fears: Being Overwhelmed, Dealing with the Unknown, Asking for Help, Not Enough Resources (e.g., time, energy, or money).

* Write an Evidence List that shows examples in your life or themes where you successfully addressed being overwhelmed, dealing with the unknown, asking for help, and gaining resources.

Exercise 3—Eight Simple Steps to Get to Good Enough

Pick an issue or a goal in your life (e.g., being impatient when things take longer than I'd like—as in all the time!).

* Rate where you are with no judgment (or as little as possible) on a scale of 1-10 (1 = lowest, 10 = highest) of how you'd like to be behaving in this scenario (e.g., 7).

* What does the least desirable scenario look like (e.g., least—I lose it regularly and people get nervous around me when I'm stressed; most—I rarely experience impatience)?

* What does Good Enough look like and what number is that (e.g., when I see myself get impatient, I'm able to stop, breathe, and calm myself down and focus on the task in front of me; that's a 2)?

* What action can you take to make that happen (e.g., plan out my day and leave extra time for things that may come up)?

* What support do you need (e.g., take fifteen minutes at the end of every day, sit calmly with a cup of tea and plan my day, and schedule an extra fifteen minutes for my top three tasks for the day)?

* How will you know when you've arrived at Good Enough (e.g., I will feel more grounded and focused during my day. I will be breathing deeper and I won't feel rushed)?

* How can you acknowledge or reward yourself for getting to Good Enough (e.g., I'll celebrate getting places on time or even early by taking out five minutes to read a book or relax)?

Check-In

* What resonated for you in this Gem?
* How can you apply it to your life?
* What is one small action you'll take NOW?

GEM 8

✳ ✳ ✳ ✳

How to Shine in Your Career

You Don't Get What You Deserve, You Get what You Negotiate

I was on a red-eye from San Francisco to LaGuardia Airport. Eyes at half-mast, I was drawn to the back page of the *Sky Mall* magazine. Its message screaming in all-caps lettering "IN BUSINESS, YOU DON'T GET WHAT YOU DESERVE, YOU GET WHAT YOU NEGOTIATE." I ripped off the back page and put it in my pocketbook. When I got home, I taped it to the cover of my box of memos. I've held on to it for twenty years. As I write this book, I'm staring at the very same tattered, but mighty, little quote that has yellowed with age, frayed at the edges, and yet the message resonates with me as much as the first time I saw it.

For us to own our SPARKLE Power, we must learn how to negotiate and advocate for ourselves. To do that, My Fabulous Fierce Ones, we must do both the inner work and take external actions.

The Price We Pay When We Don't Ask for What We Want

I was speaking at a retreat to support young women leaders when the Executive Director, Susan, shared a story that brought home the impact on the trajectory of our life when we don't ask for what we want. She shared a hypothetical yet compelling scenario in which a young man and a young woman graduate from a mid-level university with MBAs. In a perfect world, which is clearly not the case, they are both offered the same salary. Susan shared that, statistically, the guy is twice as likely to counter-offer a higher base salary than the woman, and on the average, he'll receive an additional $2,000 as his starting salary.

For most women, given the stress we experience when we negotiate for ourselves, especially right out of school, the $2,000 doesn't seem worth the bother. We opt not to "ask." We may rationalize that "we'll make it up along the way." The problem is it's never *just the two thousand dollars* but rather the cumulative effect over the life of our career. Fast forward to the end of their career, which is three-plus decades later. Susan factored into the calculations annual cost-of-living increases as well as an average 6% return on their investments (based on the man and woman putting the same money aside).

We were all slack-jawed when Susan reported that, at the time of retirement around sixty-five, the man would have $750,000 more dollars than the woman. The estimate didn't even factor in that men are promoted far more often than women, the salary gap between men and women, and rarely do they start at the same income levels. Clearly, this is a hypothetical scenario since the era of the "thirty-five years and get a gold watch" type of job are mostly a thing of the past. In addition to the fact that an average of 6% return in the market over that time period is far from common. The emotional truth does shine through. An entire lifetime of "not wanting to deal with the stress of asking" has huge impacts on all levels for women, emotionally and also financially. What can we do about it?

Adapting a Productive versus Positive Approach to Thinking

I first heard this term about a decade ago when I took Laura Berman Fortgang's, *Now What? 90 Days to a Life Direction* coaching training. When she mentioned the importance of supporting our clients to think productively versus positively, all my personal growth/professional development circuits lit up. While I'm a fan of positive thinking, I find productive thinking to be far more powerful. It urges us to ask the question, "What do we want to *produce* in our lives? What thoughts will help us get there?"

As I mentioned in the previous Gem 7 on perfectionism, when we recruit both our creativity, imagination, and pepper in a little humor, we are more able to loosen the grip that our fears have on us. We are able to connect with the resiliency and passion in every single one of us. Here is one of my favorite tools to help accomplish that.

Fears: Legitimate or Unfounded

Overall, fears get a bad rap and are largely misunderstood. Whether it's at a cocktail party, during a speaking engagement, or a conversation on the subway, I often hear my fellow humans giving ourselves a hard time when we're confronted with our fears. We either beat ourselves up for having them and try to ignore the fact that we do, or totally buy into them and believe they're all true. I know I certainly fall prey to that pattern. Granted, fears can be a very powerful force in our lives. It's understandable why we often consciously and unconsciously let them dictate the choices we make in our lives.

But just like Toto's great act of curiosity and courage revealing the true identity of the Wizard of Oz, when we peel away the layers of fears we free up our energy and our ability to make choices that support us. In doing so, we're more equipped to be able to negotiate for ourselves from a stronger stance.

Granted, there may be times where there are circumstances beyond your control such as a slow economy, geography, sexism, ageism, and technological glitches. I've worked with clients when those situations are present. All those factors can slow down our process and can frustrate us enough and make us want to give up.

> ✳ **LOIS-ism**
>
> **Sometimes our worst-case scenarios become our most valuable learning experiences.**

When that happens, I encourage them to feel those uncomfortable emotions, while being compassionate with themselves, and to *keep putting themselves out there*, while doing the internal work. I've seen it pay off. During those challenging times it's even more important to be aware of our internal dialogue. If there are fewer opportunities, you want to be on your "A" game when you do get them.

Once you tease out your fears, then there's a better chance they won't impact you in a negative way.

What started out as my worst-case scenario became one of my most valuable experiences. It was decades ago, very early in my business as a licensed medical massage therapist. I was lounging at my health club when an older woman approached my chaise. She'd been referred by her friend. She asked for my card and asked, "How much do you charge?" Being young in my business, I started to recite my perfectly memorized sales pitch. She immediately cut me off, and said, "No, no, no, none of that stuff. I just need to know your fee." I took a deep breath and told her my fee, at which she rolled her eyes and declared, rather loudly, "You're too expensive, here's your card back."

Something came over me and I started laughing hysterically. The woman glared at me and said, "What's so funny?" What came out of me shocked not only her, but me. I told her my worst fear was that someone would do exactly what she did: tell me I'm too expensive and hand me back my card. I added that in my fantasy, I had imagined that I would want to die. In reality, it was a big nothing. I thanked her for making my worst nightmare happen, only to discover that I was still here to tell the tale.

"You've given me a terrific gift." Those were the final words I said as she skulked away totally confused. I was telling the truth. Living out my "worst-case scenario fear" so early on in my business, while not pleasant, made me more resilient. It gave me perspective and the ability to lighten up. The biggest gift of all was the universe's reminder that often the horrible fantasy our mind comes up with is rarely that dramatic and terrible in real life. In realizing that, we do not have to give our fears that much power.

The punchline is that four years later, the same woman called me for a session. She was referred to me by a different person and was totally oblivious to the fact that we had met before in an uncomfortable interaction. But this time, when I told her my fee (which had gone up by about 25%) she didn't wince, get faint, or hand me back my card. She said "Okay, when can I make an appointment?" After the session, she handed me a check and said, "You're great, you don't charge enough." I had to hold myself back from laughing out loud at her reaction.

While the stakes in certain situations are much higher than others, I am reminded that often people's reactions have very little to do with us, and are usually more of a reflection of what's going on for them at the time. If we can remember that, fear will start to have less of a grip on us, and we will put ourselves in a more powerful position to advocate for ourselves. In certain cases, enjoy a big ol' belly laugh while doing it!

Feeling the Feelings is Half the Battle

One of my favorite books is *FEEL the Fear But Do It Anyway*, by Susan P. Jeffries, PhD. Twenty-plus years since it was first published, it is still the primer on dealing with fear in a productive way. To me, the most potent word in the title is *FEEL*, since it implies that when you feel or process the fear, you're more equipped to move forward. It doesn't say, "Have fear but do it anyway" or "Have fear and bully yourself into doing it anyway." The title is very intentional.

As a culture, we teach people to either implode and suppress our feelings, or explode and vent them irresponsibly, leaving us horrified by the wake of bodies we leave behind us. I know I've definitely done that in my life. To FEEL our feelings is not the same as paralysis/analysis, but to let yourself *be with* the feelings that come up, not to create a whole drama about them, but to simply *feel* them.

I know I've mentioned the importance of letting yourself feel your feelings throughout the book. I do that intentionally because as I've seen over and over, for both myself and the people in my life, that the more we do it, the more we will reap the benefits of what a transformative practice it is.

When I'm willing to experience them and let them move through my body, I'm able to shift gears much quicker and connect back with my Courage to SPARKLE. You may ask, "What does letting yourself feel your feelings have to do with learning how to negotiate for yourself?" To which I say, *"Everything."*

As women, when we go to the next level of advocating for ourselves, it's often very uncomfortable and can be really confrontational for us. It's not uncommon to feel a wash of emotions come over us as we practice unfamiliar but ultimately productive behavior.

Reframing Butterflies in Your Stomach

Except in cases of being madly in love or infatuation, or those thrill seekers who love to skydive, drive race cars, or participate in other death-defying adrenaline-based activities, most of us recoil when it comes to the experience of having "butterflies in our stomach." Yet when we are doing things that challenge us emotionally, negotiating for ourselves being at the top of the list, some of us will experience this very same feeling. We can start to reframe this experience through a positive lens.

A professional acquaintance of mine, who's always taking on the next big challenge in her life, says that if she doesn't feel butterflies in her stomach at least half the time when negotiating for herself, she knows she's not stretching herself enough. What a wonderful way to reframe the visceral experience of fear. If you look at butterflies in your stomach as a bad feeling, you'll resist it and your tension will grow. But if you can breathe and let yourself experience it as an energizing feeling, it will be transformative. Consider the fact that this feeling mostly occurs when we're about to do something that's about expansion and going beyond our Familiarity Zone.

I don't use the phrase Comfort Zone because there's nothing comfortable about staying stuck. I think the term Familiarity Zone more accurately names the complacency that sets in when we are confronted by change. Conversely, I love the phrase "butterflies in my stomach." Given the fact that butterflies epitomize transformation, we have the option to reframe that sensation as a key step in our own personal metamorphosis.

The Practicalities of Negotiating for Yourself

Along with doing the inner work of identifying your fears, concerns, and looking at best strategies for addressing them, it's time to focus on outer actions to make you a more skilled advocate for yourself.

Establish Your Top Line/Middle Line/Bottom Line

Knowing what your top and the bottom line is or what your priorities are is essential. If you have a guide for yourself, you can then powerfully choose what works and doesn't work for you. This guide is the combination of what the market rate is, what feels right for you given how much work you'll be putting in, your experience, and the type of lifestyle that is important to you. It's vital to be honest about what your skill level is. I'm not talking about second-guessing yourself, or undervaluing your services but being realistic about your levels of experience and success in particular areas. It's okay to accept the lower scale of a range if you *genuinely* feel rusty in an area and are navigating a learning curve. Make sure to be proactive about how you're going to close that gap.

If you're in your own business and create a sliding scale in your fee structure, given the population you serve, or someone's individual need at the time, make sure to have a shared agreement and expectation. For example, set a boundary (as discussed in Gem 11) that when their financial situation changes, your compensation will be adjusted accordingly. While you are the final decision-maker about what your needs are regarding salary, income, revenue or any other additional factors, I like having an established Top/Middle/Bottom Line. The Top Line is your "Wouldn't it be fabu?" wish list for a fee or salary you want to negotiate. The Middle Line is the range in which you are content, even though it may not be your top fee. The Bottom line would be a range that you can work with but that you fully intend to expand upon in the future.

Money is by far the most taboo subject on the planet. People will sooner tell you how many times they "did it," or what positions they were in when "doing it", than tell you what their salary was last year. It's still an area of great discomfort for most of us. While I think it's important to look at your needs and what you're negotiating for in a strategic and non-emotional way, I still believe feelings play an important role in negotiating for ourselves. We can have the nicest number on paper, but if we are still resentful we are going to be conflicted.

☀ LOIS-ism

Establish your RFR:
Resentment-Free Rate.

That's why several years ago, I came up with my LOIS-ism for dealing with the emotional dance that comes up in the negotiating process. I call it my Resentment-Free Rate (RFR); it's a rate that you can charge and feel absolutely resentment-free doing so. It doesn't have to be the ideal rate, but one that leaves you clear in your heart and feeling a sense of freedom. You can feel committed to doing an excellent job and not feel resentful if it involves more than you thought it would.

It's important to consider what the market will bear. Do your research and ask a few friends or colleagues who have some experience in these matters. I also think that it's equally important to honor where you are at in your life. Adopt a pricing that truly works for you, even if it makes you a little uncomfortable in service of stepping into your value. The most important, and sometimes hardest thing to do is to accept it when you pass on an opportunity or it passes on you because it is below your RFR. While difficult in the moment, you'll find great relief and create space for something in your RFR to surface. While this Gem focuses on how to negotiate for yourself and own your

✳ LOIS-ism

Educate (Don't Apologize to) Your Clients on the Value You Provide.

value from a professional perspective, all of the aforementioned principles translate seamlessly when advocating for yourself in your personal life as well.

A really great way to ask for what you want, especially financially, is to educate your clients, patients, or customers, on the exact value that you provide. This is not about defending your fees or apologizing for yourself, but rather letting them know the difference you make to the people you serve. Here are a few things to think about when educating your clients about your value:

* What do my clients, customers, or co-workers tell people about how I go the extra mile?

* What are the results that I provide to my customers?

* What might my clients not know that I can educate them about?

* How can I find out what holds the most value for them?

* How can I tie together how I go the extra mile, with how that impacts their bottom-line goals?

Let's take the example of a seller's realtor. They can say:

"I will help you sell your house."

OR

"My clients call me the 'What to expect when you're expecting to sell your house realtor.'" Usually it gets a laugh because it's a take-off of that book for first-time parents. "What I do is hold your hand every step of the way so that you can sell your house for the highest price, in the least amount of time, with as little stress as possible."

Which one do you think is most likely going to close the deal?

The first scenario simply states what they do, but the second one educates their client. I have to remind myself, as well as my clients, that our job is to educate the people we serve on the value we provide. It may feel like bragging at first, but if you focus on the "What's In It For Them," (WIIFT) factor (as my friend Peggy Klaus says) then it's not bragging, it's educating.

"Brag isn't a four-letter word."

My dear friend and colleague, Peggy Klaus, leadership and communication coach and trainer, starts many of her presentations saying that. Her best-selling book, *BRAG! The Art Of Tooting Your Horn without Blowing It* reflects the discomfort people have in bragging about themselves even in the selfie age. Known as the Brag Lady, Peggy teaches both women and men how to brag by articulating their accomplishments in Bragologues—short, pithy, conservational stories that are delivered with passion and delight. She suggests keeping a Brag Bag—a record of your accomplishments—as well as positive things that colleagues, bosses, or clients have said about you so you can draw upon them in appropriate situations. I use many of her principles when preparing clients for either interviews or to advocate for themselves when they are requesting a promotion or raise. I highly recommend her book. She goes into far greater detail in her *BRAG!* book but to give you quick dos and don'ts for bragging, she makes the following suggestions:

BAD BRAGGING

* I, I, I, Syndrome—Starting every sentence with "I did this," " I did that," which is self aggrandizing, obnoxious and boring.

* Exaggerating or lying about your accomplishments.

* Being condescending.

* One-Upmanship.

* Speaking in a Monotone.

* Always bringing the focus back to yourself versus including the other person in the conversation.

* Using the same generic soundbytes over and over.

GOOD BRAGGING.

* Short stories (Bragologues) which "show" rather than tell about your skills, talents and qualities.

* Sharing with excitement and passion what you do.

* Articulating it as a conversation versus a drive-by-monologue.

* Have varied tone and affect.

* Rehearsing specific Bragologues in a conversational tone that are specifically designed for different audiences.

One of the most important points that Peggy drives home about bragging is that women are more likely to deflect their outstanding achievements by giving all of the credit to "the team." At times, she'll get pushback where they say, "But Peggy, it's a team effort, and besides, there's no 'I' in team" thereby rationalizing that they shouldn't take any credit. Whereupon she counters, "Yes...but there's a "U" in bonus!" As women, the more skilled we become in sharing about who we are and what we're up to from a place of passion and confidence, the easier it becomes to advocate for ourselves.

LOIS-ism

It's less about what you ask for and more about how you ask for it.

While I think it's essential for women to ask for what we want, I think HOW we ask for what we want is equally, if not more, important. I often see women falling into what I call The Diva/Doormat Syndrome: a communication style that flip-flops between self-righteousness, aka The Diva, to apologizing when making requests, aka The Doormat.

LOIS-ism

Worthiness is not the same as Entitlement. Entitlement comes from a place of grandiosity and Worthiness comes from a sense of self.

Worthiness comes from self-esteem and knowing we are deserving of respect. Entitlement comes from an "I have it coming to me" attitude that makes people allergic to you and less likely to want to deal with you. When a person comes from that place of self-righteousness, their audience is turned off. In certain cases, they often freeze them out with radio silence or "stonewalling," a term used by John Gottman, one of the top relationship experts in the country. While it makes sense that one might feel entitled and diva-ish after years of feeling suppressed and undermined, it's not effective in the negotiation process. Or, it's equally common to cave in and apologize for ourselves when making requests that are stretching us past our familiarity zone. Here are some ways to overcome The Diva/Doormat Syndrome.

LOIS-ism

Avoid the Diva/Doormat Syndrome.

Request. Don't Demand or Apologize.

Tone is everything when it comes to making requests. I'm a real fan of setting boundaries with a simple, "I have a request..." and then continuing. Even if you believe it's iron-clad and it may or may not be negotiable, it's far less threatening than "You need to...." Other sentence stems I'm a fan of when coaching people how to set boundaries are:

* "What would really make a difference for me is..."
* "Let me tell you how I work so we're both clear around expectations."
* "What I've found that works best for me is..."
* "This is how I provide the most value for my clients..."
* "In order to get the most value from our work together..."

When you offer your needs as a request or as educating your clients, kids, or colleagues, the words land a lot softer and won't cause as much pushback. It's different than saying, "This is the way it's going to be." I go into further detail on boundary setting in my Gem 11—Communication that Glistens.

Ever meet someone at a party or networking event and you have to hook them up to electrodes to see if they're alive? They not only speak in a monotone but have no life force energy, are giving you a rolling resume, and you feel like you need a Red Bull in order to make it through the conversation? Yes, those folks! Make sure not to be one! Bring your *joie de vivre* to the party. Remember, enthusiasm is contagious. It's one of the few things that everyone is willing to catch!

✳ LOIS-ism

> **Get a Pulse! Enthusiasm is Contagious. It's the One Thing Most People Want to Catch!**

When your SPARKLE has gone South in Networking Situations

No matter how smart or successful we are, we all have moments in our lives where we feel off our game and not able to toot our horns in as powerful a way as we usually do. One friend felt very reluctant about going to a college reunion with her somewhat highbrow fellow alums. Even though she's very accomplished and super smart, she hit was having a temporary confidence crisis. Naturally interested in people, I suggest the magical eight words that everyone loves to hear! When faced with someone you feel intimidated by, smile and sincerely say, "You look great. Tell me all about you!" As Tim Ferriss, the best-selling author of *The Four-Hour Workweek* stated, his key strategy to connecting to the blogging community (which had a huge impact on making his book a bestseller) was to focus on being *interested* versus *interesting*.

While I do believe it's vital to create an interesting buzz about yourself, when you are genuinely interested in the other person, it relieves your nervousness and naturally connects you to people in a rich and genuine way. Years later, I'm continually reminded that with all the training I've had, my most effective and natural sales approach is to say, "Tell me all about you," and, "How can I help you?" and *mean* it.

✳ LOIS-ism

Don't Tap Dance Around Your Power-- Own it!

Would you ever opt to watch two TV shows on a split screen with two totally different messages being conveyed at the same time? Probably not! It would be confusing and make it hard to focus. It's the same experience when our words and behavior are giving out two totally different messages. From time to time, we may unknowingly have given out mixed messages. I see it the most when I work with women advocating for themselves. They will have a rock star resume, possess all the smarts, savvy to negotiate what they want, and may be very well "put together," but then they'll use "qualifiers" that undermine their expertise and credibility. They'll say things like:

* "I'm not sure this is right but..."

* "Not to insert my opinion, however..."

* "Not to interrupt, but..."

In addition, there's a host of words that undermine our value:

* Perhaps.

* Maybe.

* Hopefully.

Followed by a series of "Sorry, Sorry, Sorry, Sorry."

When I give my clients that feedback, they'll shake their heads knowing they do it, but often add, "I just don't want to come across as too aggressive or full of myself."

There is definitely a double standard of how women and men are perceived. As women, we do need to finesse our communication styles accordingly; especially when it comes to expressing our needs and advocating for ourselves. For example, a man who speaks his mind is called strong and decisive, whereas if a woman's tone is off, she may be perceived as aggressive and strident. Double standards obviously do exist. However, there's no reason that women can't find a firm and friendly style that states who we are, what we are up to, and advocates for ourselves in a clear and effective manner. Getting rid of qualifiers is an important step toward that. To learn more about how to use words that empower you, watch my YouTube SMART SEXY TV episode called *"Don't Tap Dance around Your Power; Own It!"*

Culture Shopping—Finding Your Tribe in the Workplace

What I find to be pretty universal is when people work with their tribe, they are pretty content. There will be times where they are no longer stimulated by what they do or they need to move on. By and large, I do find that when people are in a work culture that suits them, their job satisfaction goes up exponentially.

I suggest to everyone that when you go on an interview, show up fifteen to twenty minutes early, hang out, and pay attention. You'll find out way more about the culture than what most interviewers will reveal. Look at the décor, how the receptionist greets you and is being treated, how co-workers interact with each other, and the overall vibe. Your body will let you know whether it's "yum" or "yuck," or "still not sure."

Many clients who initially felt they had to change professions or industry, learned what they really craved was working in a culture they felt aligned with. Below are the categories of cultures that I see most work environments fall under. I've included a brief description next to each and see if you recognize your own. Feel free to add some that come to you. Most work cultures are a combination of one or more the following characteristics.

* **Growth Focused**—Cultures that support expansion, risk, personal initiative, and advancement.

* **Adrenaline-Based**—Intense, long hours, rewarding risk-taking activity, and often drama.

* **Compliant**—Emphasizes following the rules above creativity and innovation.

* **Relational**—Focused on building the relationship amongst team members.

* **Wholesome**—People get along but are not always growth- and expansion-focused.

* **Connected**—Relationships are intact and are long-standing.

* **Disconnected**—High levels of isolation and working in your own silo.

* **Egregious**—Snarky and barbed humor and behavior are rewarded.

* **Toxic**—An emotional minefield of harassment, where one day something flies and the next you'll get your head blown off for it.

In cases where you work for yourself and are a team of one, it's equally important to assess your personal, desired culture. I have clients who are solo-preneurs and small business owners. Even though they work for themselves, they prefer to be around other people or they feel isolated. Others need more solitary time. It's a very individual preference.

Sometimes departments and teams have sub-cultures within the company, or as I said, they can be a combination. The most important thing is to assess both the culture you are in and what culture allows you to thrive.

Case in point: I had a client who was in the healthcare field. She had planned to quit and travel because she was exhausted and dreaded going to work. After some consideration, she realized that if she quit she'd come back six months later to the same situation, only poorer. As she looked deeper, her version of "wanting to run away to the circus" was largely fueled by her need to escape the toxicity in her work culture. She was not only treated horribly but her company was doing things that were unethical, and she felt trapped. Through a series of sessions, we identified the culture that would best suit her. She realized she would do well in a growth-focused company that would utilize her entrepreneurial talents. She still wanted the steadiness of a paycheck, so a hybrid of a growth-focused and relational culture was her best fit.

Six months later she made a lateral move, something that would not have been exciting earlier but that she now considered a giant jump in her job satisfaction. While her income only increased by 10%, she was treated like the superstar she is. She was constantly asked for her input, regularly invited into the meetings with the "higher ups," and given a robust benefits and vacation package so she could still travel—something she loved.

For the first few sessions after her job started, she'd report in an almost shocked tone, "They really respect my expertise and are always telling me what a difference I make." Clearly, she had felt so beaten up by her former work culture that being in one that was aligned with who she was still surprised her. She was relieved not to have to change industries and to have some extra time to pursue her artistic passions.

Consider the Work Culture You're In

There's a very big difference between feeling suppressed because you can't be your most authentic self in your work culture, and understanding that you may need to shift your behavior or style of communication as a strategy to gain a connection with your community. For example, if you're a rabble-rouser but you're in a deeply compliant culture all about rules and not about innovation, you'll consistently be seen as a troublemaker. You'll feel criticized and suppressed. If there are enough perks at the job that you don't want to leave, you'll need to find small, non-threatening ways to express this desire at your workplace. Or, you will need to address those needs outside of your work culture. When you consciously make that choice for the bigger goal, it will give you freedom and perspective. If you see it as consistently being suppressed, then you'll continue to feel frustrated and inauthentic. It's really about how you see it and then powerfully choosing, based on what's most important to you in your life.

REFLECTION CHECK-IN

* What type of work culture do you thrive in?

* What type of work culture are you in, right now?

* How might you need to adjust either the way you communicate or behave?

* What small action can you take to become more aligned with your work culture?

Supporting Your Team's SPARKLE

I've seen many examples of different leaders who have leveraged their team's SPARKLE in a brilliant and impeccable way. The one that affected me most was my first-hand account at the tender age of sixteen. It was one of my first jobs and I was working at a nationwide ice cream parlor. I was a real schmoozer. I'd joke with the kids, make up voices and play games with them. Since we pooled tips, the other workers weren't thrilled with me even though I still worked very hard. However, lots of rules trigger my Audacious Girl, who loves adventure and spontaneity and is not a fan of being told what to do. Plus, I was a huge Cyndy Lauper fan and my anthem was (and still is), "Girls Just Want to Have Fun."

There was not a lot of room for fun in this joint, even though the thought of a humorless ice cream parlor still amazes me today. Ice cream is fun! But in this store, you had to make sure you had exactly the right initials when referring to everything; Mint Chocolate Chip was MCC, nothing else but MCC. Lots of rules; lots of chores; lots of clean up.

The manager was a lovely guy who, while being laid-back, was quite attuned to his staff. One Easter, everyone poured in after church. There were lines out the door and lots of crying babies. We were short-staffed and sweating it. I'll never forget what he did. He took me off the floor, got me a few plastic hand puppets that were giveaways, moved all the families with young screaming children into the same section, and told me to put on a puppet show in the middle of rush hour.

The other employees started to bitch. "Why does she get to have fun while we're working hard? We shouldn't have to split tips with her."

He shook his head and said, "You people don't understand. Lois is working just as hard—even harder, in fact, because she's under more pressure. Her work just looks different. If we don't quiet the kids down, three-quarters of the restaurant will be so irritated they'll leave and we'll be twiddling our thumbs for the rest of the day. Do you want that?"

Of course, they all shook their heads, "No."

"But if she quiets the kids down and entertains them, then everyone will be happy and we can accommodate the rush and make more money and everyone's happy." Reluctantly, everyone agreed.

Step-by-step, he threw away the official manual and broke all the rules. He moved everyone on the team around and put them in positions that highlighted their strengths. One girl, who was crazy fast and knew the keys by heart, was put on the cash register. He utilized the big guy who could carry eight sundaes on a tray by leveraging his sweat equity. He moved the other girl, who knew exactly where all fifty-five flavors were and could recite the initials in her sleep, to head scooper.

An entire third of the restaurant with screaming kids was moved over to my section and were transfixed by my puppet show. Instead of crying, they were literally squealing with delight. The parents were beyond grateful for the reprieve. Other people came by to listen. The rest of the team were on fire because they were utilizing best skills and what they enjoyed doing most. We felt like superstars. We were like this fast-food fireworks show that was lighting up the sky.

Customers felt our energy and focus. That day, I learned the magic that's possible when, as Jim Collins, the author of *Good to Great,* says, you put the *right people* in the *right seat* on the *right bus*: the bus moves on its own. While it may be important for employees to expand their skill sets and stretch themselves, it's a far more effective strategy to celebrate how each person on your team shines. When you put your team in positions where their natural talents can burn brightly, they get to celebrate the multi-faceted gems that they are and everyone wins!

Pay attention to your team and the people you work with. Stop harping on their weaknesses. Amplify their strengths and give them projects that highlight them. Look at what puts them on Dimmers and what lights them up. Have lunch together and start asking them to share something they are passionate about or which project was their favorite one and why. We're all so over-extended that we stop being aware of the gifts and passions of the people around us. It's time to stop, breathe, look around, notice, and do something active about what we find. While business and company structure has changed *dramatically* since my teens, the foundational principle of supporting your team's SPARKLE is an evergreen one that shines through decades later.

Let's Change the Way We Speak about Ourselves and Other Women!

Language transforms perception. We can intentionally choose to use productive and supportive language that celebrates women going after their dreams. In doing so, we can begin to shift the old, outdated paradigm and double standard that clearly exists. We must get on board as a gender and make a collective decision to do so.

I was delighted when I recently received a tweet from an influential, on-line women's entrepreneurial group created by Millennials. I'm paraphrasing, but it stressed the importance of substituting the word *ambitious* for *aggressive* when speaking about women who ask for what they want and go after their dreams.

I tweeted back. "Great, let's add to the list *unstoppable, feisty, courageous, gutsy, adventurous* and *worthy*!" Listing those words lifted my energy.

If we can start to look at how we've internalized those messages and focus on how we can change that conversation, both on an individual and collective level, we can shift that paradigm.

I once heard a man speak about how his wife brings Technicolor to his black-and-white life. The whole room of women lit up in response. When we embrace self-love and spend more time bringing to our family and community what makes us SPARKLE, we elevate not only ourselves but the world around us. Advocating for ourselves and putting ourselves out there sends an important message to our SPARKLE-Sistas, it transforms us, the world, and helps us embrace life as the extraordinary adventure that it is!

EXERCISES

✳   ✳   ✳   ✳

Exercise 1—Reframing Butterflies in Your Stomach

The next time you have butterflies in your stomach try these steps:

* ✳ STOP. Don't distract yourself by trying to avoid the feeling.

* ✳ Breathe into it, and get curious about what the sensation feels like. Is there a color or texture to the tension? Are there any images? On a level of intensity between 1-10, what number is it?

* ✳ Keep breathing.

* ✳ Close your eyes and visualize yourself as the butterfly who is literally spreading her wings and taking off. It may be before a performance, presentation, asking your boss for a raise, or a challenging conversation with someone. In this interaction, you're doing something unfamiliar and new so take a moment to acknowledge that. When you think in expansive images, it lessens the contractive nature of fear and you'll feel energized and less anxious.

* ✳ Ask yourself, "What do I need right now?"

* ✳ If you're dealing with negative self-talk, go to my SMART SEXY TV "Itty Bitty Committee" Exercise episode. Go through the easy-to-follow three step process.

* ✳ If you're emotionally triggered and you want to de-stress, go to my SMART SEXY TV and check out my episode on "Un-Trigger Your Stress in Five Minutes or Less."

✳ Do what comes naturally to you. I'm an audio (hearing) kinesthetic (feeling) learner. I need to talk out loud and move in order to let my "butterflies" move through me. Maybe you're more visual, visualizing something pleasant and expansive may hold more value for you. Play with it and make it your own.

Exercise 2—Fear Inventory

There is a tremendous power in actually writing down your fears about what you're negotiating for. You can journal about them or list them on paper.

Examples

✳ "If I ask for what I want, I won't get it."

✳ "This is my only chance. I better take what I can and make sure they like me, otherwise, I won't have other opportunities."

✳ "I'm overqualified. I better play down my skills or they'll never give me the job."

Are They Legitimate?

Some fears are absolutely legitimate. They have some possibility of happening.

Example of a legitimate fear: "If I ask for what I want, I won't get it." In this case, there's a 50% chance that you won't. But the power of seeing it on paper is to say, "And I'll have 0% chance of getting it if I don't ask."

Are They Unfounded?

Example of an unfounded fear: "This is my only chance. I better take what I can and make sure they like me, otherwise, I won't have other opportunities." It's easy to see that this one is unfounded because there's never a "last chance." If you remain in motion toward your goals and look for opportunities to move forward, they will show up.

What's powerful about writing down your fears is your inner debater/advocate can see them. They have a chance to challenge them and say, "Hey wait a minute, that doesn't make sense!" or "That's ridiculous!" "You'll find a way to strategize and address a legitimate fear in an effective way." For example:

"I'm overqualified so I better play down my skills or they'll never give me the job." Fear of being overqualified for a job is a legitimate fear. Some employers are concerned if you are overqualified, you may use the job as a steppingstone and leave. Then they will have to spend time and money re-training someone to replace you. Knowing that it's a legitimate fear, you can develop some strategies like:

* Sharing how your vision is aligned with the mission of the company.

* Talking about new opportunities and markets that you're passionate about getting into, therefore, you're open to taking a possible salary reduction.

* Expressing different skill sets you're looking to develop.

Check-In

* ✳ What resonated for you in this Gem?

* ✳ How can you apply it to your life?

* ✳ What is one small action you'll take NOW?

GEM 9

✳ ✳ ✳ ✳

FROM DIMMERS TO SHIMMERS

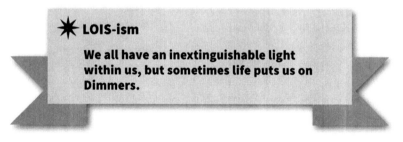

✳ **LOIS-ism**

We all have an inextinguishable light within us, but sometimes life puts us on Dimmers.

How to Make the Little Things Not Turn into the Big Things

I'm amazed how often it's the little things in life that put us on Dimmers. I remember one day that epitomized this. I had a writing deadline on an article, a slew of business actions to follow up on, a time-sensitive proposal, and several back-to-back coaching clients. I was on the conveyer belt of life, one thing after another, but somehow doing fine. I was in the flow, navigating several things and moving forward on important goals.

All of a sudden, my computer froze. I tried everything. I shut it off, I turned it on. I hit every key that had worked in the past. I simply couldn't reboot it. Even worse, I couldn't reboot myself. I started screaming at the computer and was suddenly so enraged at it that I briefly entertained the fantasy of throwing it out the window, like that would have accomplished anything.

At that moment, I had a "split screen existence." I was both in the scene and watching the scene; immersed in a dual reality. On one screen I'm screaming at my computer and losing it. On the other screen, my witness self points out, "You do know the computer is not really alive, right?" One sure sign I'm on Dimmers is when I am screaming at an inanimate object.

Most women I know, both personally and professionally, are pretty adept at dealing with intense challenges. Then some annoying but relatively inconsequential thing happens and we lose it. I hear over and over again: "I should be above this?" "Why am I letting something so silly get to me?" I've asked myself all those same questions at one point or another.

What I find is that if we don't address the little things, they quickly become the big things. They can range from small, costly annoyances like the late parking ticket, to more serious issue of pulling an all-nighter before a deadline to—worse—having a few weeks of neglecting your body turn into a flat-on-your-back setback. We've all had those experiences in life. Before we know it, we're on Dimmers! We're disconnected from our most vital and engaged self, from what makes us SPARKLE.

The Myth of "Work-Life Balance"

I was doing a training with a branch of the federal government when a conservatively dressed man in his late 50s approached me. In a no-nonsense way, he said, "I hope you'll be addressing work-life balance in your talk, it's of utmost importance." I walked away, shocked. The pendulum had officially swung. Work-life balance, usually considered a "woman's issue," is now an equal opportunity torment that leaves unanswered the deeper question, "How do I slow down enough to clarify, let alone honor, my priorities?"

I've never ascribed to the concept of work-life balance. It has always felt like a totally unrealistic goal. The image of work-life balance as a scale that has an ideal fixed point. Every aspect of our life weighs in and is perfectly coordinated with our priorities, both a personal and professional level. That's simply not the way life works! I like to think of it as *work-life integration* that factors in the different elements of our life in a comprehensive way. At certain times one or more areas of our life will eclipse the others. The most important aspect is that one is making a conscious choice that still considers the remaining areas while being in line with the larger goals.

Fast-forward to the second month of that training where I asked the group to share their victories. The same gentleman stood up, and in the most nonplussed manner, told me his marriage got better. When I asked him how that occurred, he told me that all he did was to arrive on time every night for dinner. "Somehow," the rest of the night went really well. When I asked him what changed that allowed him to come home on time, he shrugged and murmured "nothing much." He said he simply made a commitment to do so. All of the women in the room broke into laughter. They saw him making the choice to commit was *exactly* what had shifted the outcome. What he called a "better work-life balance" was really a decision to put his marriage first and then identifying a small but significant action that accomplished that goal.

Now for many of you, this scenario may feel too simplistic. I use it because I have seen that what feels like this huge quest for work-life fit often comes down to making a few foundational changes and sticking with them. We can get distracted with fancy work-life systems. There are many issues that may need to be addressed. We often forget that the simple act of making consistent choices that align with your goals, paves the way for a more fulfilling life. There's no right or wrong way to go about it but what's right for you in your life, right now.

> ✳ **LOIS-ism**
>
> **What did the police say to the therapist whose apartment got robbed? "Ma'am, it clearly looks like an inside job." The therapist nodded back in an all too knowing way and responded, "Officer, it's *always* an inside job."**

REFLECTION CHECK-IN

* ✳ What are the three most important things in your life, right now?
* ✳ What is a small but consistent action that, if you take on a regular basis, will move you toward that goal?
* ✳ How will making that goal create a better work-life fit?
* ✳ When will you take that action?

From Dimmers...

Here are the major ways that life put us on Dimmers, and what we can do to reconnect with a sense of purpose and passion, a state I call "Shimmers."

> ✳ **LOIS-ism**
>
> **Variety is the spice of life, but if you're always reminding yourself of what you're missing out on, it can become the vice of life.**

The bad news is that we take ourselves with us wherever we go. The good news is that we take ourselves with us wherever we go. We're clearly the common denominator in our lives. I call it Planet Moi. When we take responsibility (versus blaming ourselves) for our reactions, we can move from Dimmers to Shimmers with greater ease and a sense of personal power.

Avoiding the Compare/Despair Trap

I put this category first because nothing kills off our natural exuberance and vitality more than comparing ourselves to others. There is no win-win in either one-upmanship or one-downmanship. Everybody loses. With all these seemingly Pinterest-perfect lives that so many people purport to have, the theme of compare/despair has become systemic in our society and in the world.

Here's the four most common ones I've witnessed in the compare/despair category, many of which, I've struggled with in my life. I continually witness these in both my professional work as well as with my friends and colleagues. Here are several of the most powerful techniques and principles that not only I, but the people I work with, have used that help us to move from Dimmers to Shimmers.

Fear of Missing Out (FOMO)

My mom, Edie, was the FOMO Queen; more in the mundane than the magical part of life. Whether it was my going to a thrift shop or decluttering my apartment, her initial response was always the same: "Gee, Lo, that sounds great. Was there anything I may have missed out on? Hope you didn't give away anything I would have wanted!" Right underneath the surface, she was saddened by the possibility of missing out on ...something. Like Edie, if I'm not careful, I can easily become the FOMO Princess.

We will always be missing out. Not because our life isn't fabulous but because we're mere mortals and life is not a sci-fi movie. We can't clone and place ourselves in parallel universes and do seventeen things at once. We can't experience everything we might want to. You may see your friend recently got back from a safari, while you are still in timeshare tyranny and all that's left is that crappy condo in Atlantic City. Or, you're knee-deep in climbing out of clutter while your colleague is taking a helicopter ride with the Dalai Lama. Or, there are five events you want to go to at the same time but you need to stay home and work. The internet, especially social media, can spark a frantic FOMO in some of us who are news junkies. The biggest tragedy of FOMO is that it prevents you from appreciating the gifts in your own life and prevents you from being present with them and yourself.

Here are a few things that will help you loosen the grip that FOMO has on your life:

Know and understand your priorities, both personal and professionally. When you are crystal clear on what your core priorities are that inspire you, then you'll be less likely to be affected by FOMO. If you're in a period where you're inundated by a project that you don't enjoy but needs to get done, think of the bigger picture and the relief you'll experience once it's completed. We experience joy when we're clear about what matters in our lives and are taking steps to live a life that lights us up. I love options and will always be a variety junkie, but there is a tremendous serenity that comes from simplicity.

Be Clear about what Effort something REALLY Takes, not what you Think it would Take

Most of us are totally unrealistic about how long or how much work something takes both on a logistical and mental bandwidth level.

As a kid, I had been to many to auctions so I thought it would be really cool to be an auctioneer; not for a full-time profession, but just on the side for extra income. Coincidentally several years back, a friend recommended me as an auctioneer for an arts organization fundraiser. They wanted me to include my comedy in the event. To their amazement, and quite frankly to mine, I had a blast and it was a blazing success.

My friend, seeing me in action, encouraged me to do more auctioneering. I started to get really excited. I had no interest in it being a full-time gig but for a little extra income it was appealing. I had no idea how to pursue it, but I had an aunt who was a very well established antique dealer in New York City. She sent me off to the "real" auctions where established auctioneers work. I also did a little research, to discover not only the fierce competition but the elaborate training involved. In addition, I learned that when thousands (sometimes millions) of dollars are on the line, the *last thing* the serious auction houses wanted was having a comedic spin. If I had been truly passionate about it, and wanted it to be a full-time profession, I would've gone for it. Clearly that was not the case.

Instead of being disappointed, I was delighted. I was able to cross it off my "great ways to make some extra income" list because I found out, it wasn't for me. We need to get a real sense of not only the time something takes but also of the amount of energy and money.

Do a motive check-in (where is your FOMO coming from?)
I'm a huge believer in doing regular motive check-ins to identify the motivations behind your feelings and what prompts them. What is your motivation? Why does this truly interest you?

When my clients struggle with FOMO, they often find the roots being insecurity and not measuring up. For example, "I have to do that training because I don't really believe I know enough, or I'm not good enough." That's very different from honestly assessing your skill set and seeing where you need to upgrade your knowledge, based on what the market demand is. Start to notice how your body feels when you experience FOMO. I go straight to feeling a sense of lack, my body contracts, and I get anxious. Other people flood with anger and feel overwhelmed, confused, like they're "doing their life wrong." Knowing how you're wired allows you to unwire. In doing so, you'll move from Dimmers to Shimmers.

If you Still Long to do Something, Work it into your Schedule

If after you go through all the aforementioned steps, you still discover you have longings for a particular event or goal, find a way you can work it into your life.

One colleague of mine hungered to live in the country but couldn't afford it and didn't want to do it alone. She just wasn't ready to take it on. Instead, she volunteered at a local garden in New York City and had her own patch of paradise. She shared her joy of making beautiful meals and flavoring them with the spices that she had grown herself. Later when her family's run-down country cabin became available, she totally transformed it into a jewel. Her family was beyond delighted and what had been a ramshackle eye-sore is now a respite in which her family can connect.

> ✳ **LOIS-ism**
>
> **EN-SPIRATION: Use Envy as a guide to create a life that IN-SPIRES You.**

I find the experience of feeling envious is less about wanting *exactly* what the other person has and more about how we believe it will *feel* to have those things. For example, while people may envy an uber-wealthy person like Bill Gates or Warren Buffet or big time celebrities, chances are they don't want that exact life. The thought of that level of responsibility, lack of privacy, or sheer decades of work, risks, and sacrifices involved to get there, is not something that speaks to the envier. However, when

I probe deeper about what appeals to them, they'll use words like "recognition," "being an innovator," "financial freedom," "adventure," and so on. When you peel away the layers to the core values or feelings you desire, you're more likely to be able to replicate those elements in your life, right now.

The Front is Not the Back

Recently, I was at a networking event. I met this woman who was an assistant to one of most well-established experts in Human Development. This expert had the whole package: charisma, smarts, kindness, financial success, and is very spiritual. Deeply enamored, I asked her what it was like to work for a nationally known icon, a brilliant pioneer. The assistant was very professional, as she should be, but gave cryptic responses like "interesting" and "growth-enhancing." I knew something was not being addressed. I kept poking away and she finally cracked. With a weak smile, she said, "The front is not the back."

"The front is not the back," is a phrase that has stayed with me ever since. When I'm drowning in a sea of compare and despair, I see it as a spiritual life preserver that keeps me afloat. I know I'm not alone.

Here's a few things to think about:

Acknowledge When You're Triggered

This goes back to the importance of honoring your wiring that I discuss in Gem 6. Learning to identify what goes on in your body and your emotions when you're triggered, allows you to not react to it. What does it look and feel like for you? Do you get small and start apologizing for yourself? Or, maybe you start competing and bragging to level the playing field? Or, maybe your stomach gets knotty and your shoulders get tight. Start to notice.

Don't Make Assumptions

Remind yourself that you're hearing information from a very skewed source, most of which, is largely inaccurate or doesn't include the full story. It's not about begrudging someone else's success, it's about staying focused and regaining your own sense of equanimity.

Ask Questions

I love to ask questions when I'm confronted by this particular issue and I remind my clients to do the same. Just because someone spins something a certain way, doesn't mean it's the true reality. When you ask questions, you'll not only learn more but understand the real deal. You're not shooting them down or sparring with them, but uncovering what the real facts are in a "tell me more" kind of way.

Don't Compare your Insides to Someone Else's Outsides

This, to me, is one of the most brilliant slogans that I learned from twelve-step programs. Having worked with many an icon, both in the sports and entertainment field, believe me, "the front is not the back." Don't do that to yourself!

We are all connected. We can transform what triggers us from what we *perceive* others have and instead use it as an indicator of what inspires us. We can both be happy for their success while reminding ourselves that we are on our own track.

Energy Drainers

While Dimmers and Shimmers are particular mindsets, Energy Gainers and Energy Drainers are specific ways of how we focus our energy, which is our greatest resource. I can be very tired and low energy, then I run into a friend I haven't seen for a while and really perk up. Speaking with people I enjoy is an example of an Energy Gainer. While most of us have very busy lives, much of our exhaustion comes from suppressing our energy, truth, and vitality, rather than expressing it. Below is a list of the most common ones I hear.

Common Energy Drainers

* Dealing with negative and toxic people.
* Technological breakdowns.
* Clutter.
* Being stuck in traffic.
* Doing tasks that we're not good at that need to get done.

If we identify the Energy Drainers/Energy Gainers in our lives and use these valuable insights to reconnect with our natural enthusiasm for life, it will make all the difference in the world. We can take ourselves from Dimmers ... **To Shimmers**

Energy Gainers

My friend Peggy, who doesn't even live in New York City, sees more Broadway, opera, and cultural events than most New Yorkers I know. Immersing herself in all forms of art is a huge Energy Gainer for her. What does your list look like? I can guarantee that if you take an action, big or small, to eliminate an Energy Drainer and integrate an Energy Gainer every week, you'll be far more skilled in navigating the Dimmers and moving into Shimmers.

Another example: Bonding with strangers is one of my major Energy Gainers. I *love* bonding with strangers. I don't mean the occasional "Boy, it's bad weather" chit-chat, that holds little to no interest for me. I mean everything from occasionally breaking into song in an elevator and having another person join in, to sitting down for an hour to hear about someone's early childhood years in Haiti. People's lives and journeys fascinate me, and therefore, enhance my energy.

Bonding with *everyone all the time* is not something I would want to do. However when I am on Dimmers, a quick Energy Gainer of striking up a conversation with a stranger does the trick. Last month, I was feeling stressed out by all the things I had to accomplish. I took the subway on my way to getting things done. Across from me was a guy playing harmonica for his own enjoyment. He paused for a moment. I asked him a few basic questions about how long he had been playing. He went into detail about his love/hate relationship with the harmonica. While he loved the sound, the convenience, and that it was such an accessible and affordable instrument, the restrictive nature of the instrument saddened him. There were genres of music that he would never be ever considered for, classical music, being one of them, even though he loved it and was quite good at it.

I asked him what instrument he thought he was in the orchestra of life, and he became intrigued. I watched other passengers start to ponder that question to themselves. I included them in the discussion and an impromptu, albeit brief, connection formed between several of us. I had lost track of the time and place. When my stop came and I had to jump off quickly; one person called out, "Don't leave! We just got started." What had begun as a stressed-out morning, turned into an energized and productive afternoon. I was reminded of how we all crave more connection and the powerful effect that Energy Gainers can have on our lives.

Below is a list of the most common ones I hear.

Common Energy Gainers

* Snuggle time with your partner.
* Taking fifteen minutes and reading a good book.
* Walking briskly in nature.
* Laughing with friends.
* Meditation or some mindful practice.
* Creative time (e.g., knitting, cooking, painting).

The Importance of Staying in Your Own Lane

I love the metaphor of *Staying in Your Own Lane*. We're often driving at high speeds like we do in life every day. We have a much better chance of enjoying the scenery, not crashing into another person, when we stay focused on what we're moving toward in our own life.

One day when I was overwrought, I watched myself get off-course, too focused on what other people were doing. I stopped, breathed, and reminded myself, "Lois, stay in your own lane." Then it occurred to me: my lane is the *Lois Lane*: the quickest route to a Super Life. We all have our own lane that leads us to a Super Life, and we must stay in it!

Honor What You Do Know

Karol Ward is an Inner Confidence Expert, speaker, coach, psychotherapist, and a dear friend of mine. One of her key pieces of advice that she shares with both clients and friends is, "You know what you know." We all have so much brilliance within us that, if we stay open, we are guided to where we need to go. Learning to listen and trust ourselves takes practice, like everything else. The more we do it, the more confident we get. There's a tremendous pleasure and ease to life when we can truly trust, listen to, and honor ourselves. You know what you know. Living a life that lights us up is truly an inside job.

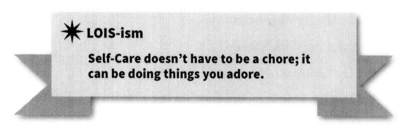

LOIS-ism

Self-Care doesn't have to be a chore; it can be doing things you adore.

Sassy Self-Care

Almost every month in every women's magazine, there is a new system, approach, chart, ten books to read, or a check-list for best strategies on dealing with self-care. I'm a total human development geek and a self-help hobbyist by both nature and profession. While I enjoy it immensely, if I overdo it I can start to feel like *I'm* the damn project rather than a person who is passionate about living her life to the fullest and helping others to do the same.

I'd suggest you give your self-care a name that inspires you. I call mine Sassy Self-Care! In an effort to override my propensity for terminal earnestness, I adore feeling sassy. Being sassy to me encompasses being bold, irreverent, audacious, flirty, and playful. Just saying "Sassy Self-Care" boosts up my *joie de vivre* and puts me on Shimmers.

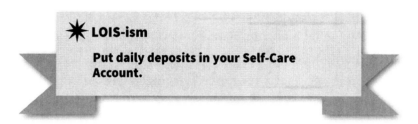

LOIS-ism

Put daily deposits in your Self-Care Account.

At certain junctures of your life, self-care may need to be on a more formal and structured level. At other times, it may need to be more loose and free-floating. Be creative, have fun, and be realistic about what connects you to your natural life force energy. It's far better to start small and build than to be overly ambitious and bail three minutes later. The goal of self-care is to connect with your essential self, and you get to choose the specific type of nurturing care that you need. I have to do something creative every day, or else I'm on Dimmers. It may be sharing a story with a client that can teach them something, writing, or just walking in nature. Creativity and art are one of the great gifts in life, which is why a lot of my self-care revolves around my creativity. Otherwise, I turn into a cranky pants. Honor what's important to you.

While I enjoy integrating different adventures into my life and view them as self-care (e.g. thrift shops, conversations with strangers, reading, singing, dancing, learning), there are four core areas that are fundamental to maintaining a healthy lifestyle. But I still don't want it to feel boring.

Keeping Track of the Basics

Given my motto, "another day another acronym," I created a simple tracking system which I call FEMS: Food, Exercise, Mindfulness, and Sleep. I track all four in a very simple way. I am a low/no tech person, I write mine by hand in a journal. I know there are countless apps out there for you tech-savvy folks where you can design your own tracking system of what puts you on Shimmers. Do what works for you.

Since my self-care must include the basics to maintain a fairly healthy lifestyle (given a zippy name) but also be broad enough to include creativity, socializing, and adventure, my FEMS tracking system is pretty simple. Next to each category, I have a few specific criteria that I like to log in order to make sure I'm on track:

* **Food:** What did I eat?
* **Exercise:** What did I do? (Dance Class? 10K steps? Core?)
* **Mindfulness:** What did I do? (Meditation, Journaling, Gratitude Journal, anything that slows down the monkey mind is in the mindfulness category.)
* **Sleep:** When did I go to bed? How many hours? Was it restful?

At the bottom of the page, I have a simple "Note to Self" section where I write my insights for the day. It could be anything from navigating my relationship with self-care, an insight/LOIS-ism, or a challenge that I'm having and need to address. Two or three sentences tops! It keeps me present.

I have performance margins where I can improve in all of those areas. I'm fairly well-rested and in "good enough" shape. Three decades later, I've maintained a thirty-five-pound weight loss while not being too neurotic about food (you know what I'm talking about). Considering where I came from, all of this is substantial progress.

Like everyone, I love getting a gold star and I derive an almost freakish pleasure from checking off those boxes. At the end of the week, I make sure that my total is in the 80/20 ratio. Meaning 80% of the time, I'm in the "good enough" category of food, exercise, mindfulness, and sleep.

When I have a wash of a week when I don't track, I know my priorities are off and I need to make an adjustment. I take a moment to see what prevented me from doing it and return to my system. I've been doing it for a while and it keeps me pretty consistent.

Many people gain great benefits from on-line support and a community associated with their digital tracking. Others like me, are more invested in paper and a few good support buddies. It's whatever works. Consistency and workability are more important than making these huge declarations and then falling short, feeling like you've let yourself down. When we take the time to care for ourselves, not only do we bring more of our SPARKLE to our work and life but we become more tuned-in and open to inner guidance. It is a very important element of learning to trust ourselves.

Develop a Morning Ritual that Nurtures Your Spiritual Connection

How you start your day impacts how you navigate your day, emotionally as well as logistically. When we start our day "on the right foot," it sets a precedent for putting one foot in front of the other for the rest of the day. That's why I suggest that you bring at least a piece of your Sassy Self-Care to your mornings whenever possible. It will set the tone for the rest of the day. I have a friend who leaves the house for work by 7:00 a.m. No matter what she takes an additional fifteen minutes to read spiritual or inspiring quotes and literature during/before a brief stroll through her illustrious garden. She calls it her spiritual medicine for the day. Given she works in a stressful environment, "taking her spiritual medicine" every day allows her easy-going calm manner to serve her, no matter what chaos is going on around her. She's been doing it for decades and says she treats it like brushing her teeth. She'd NEVER leave the house without doing it!

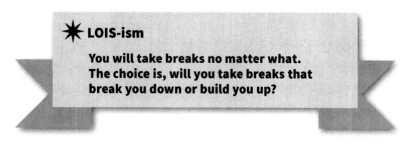

LOIS-ism

You will take breaks no matter what. The choice is, will you take breaks that break you down or build you up?

Break Points

Whenever I refuse to give myself a break from an intense workflow or a situation, my body does the slowing down for me. When I look back, I see that most of those mishaps that caused my injuries could have been avoided if I had just taken more breaks and paid more attention. I also see this pattern with my clients. When they get sick or feel temporarily disabled, it usually is caused by days, weeks, or even months of pushing themselves too hard.

Do Your "Breaks" Tune You In or Zone You Out?

Examples of zoning out include: mindless TV that is either numbing, violent, or mean-spirited; surfing the net; overspending; drinking; overeating junk food; engaging in conversations that deteriorate friendships—and so on. The difficulty with zoning-out breaks is they are often fueled by addiction, diminish intimacy, and do anything but revitalize you. Ultimately, taking breaks is for rejuvenating you and rebooting your energy and focus. It is just as important to look at what you are using your breaks for (avoid and hide out, or connect and reboot) as it is to consider the actual activities you choose.

Breaks That Help You Tune In

I was working with a client who was drafting a very important document for an influential figure in banking. She worked all night. When I later came to her home to do a session, her bed was covered with trashy romance novels. We have a very transparent relationship with each other, so I said, "Wow, I'd never think *you* would read this stuff." She smiled back and said, "I've been writing for twelve hours straight. What do you think I'm going to read for entertainment—*War and Peace*?" We both laughed. She was very clear that numbing herself with mindless romance novels was her way of rebooting—*after* finishing the task on time. The difference is she did it consciously as a reward and her "recreational reading" was a way to lighten up, given the heavy nature of the document she was drafting.

When working on deciphering the difference between a tuning-in and zoning-out break, your Energy Drainers/Energy Gainers list can come in really handy. Look for ways that you can build your Energy Gainers into your life. When you're dealing with times that you are going through a major transition, eliminate an Energy Drainer when dealing with a task that requires a fair amount of mental and emotional bandwidth.

Self-Soothing versus Self-Numbing

This principle is in the same family as Tuning-In versus Zoning-Out but subtly different. As children, very few of us were taught how to soothe ourselves. This a product of our culture and one's own self-parenting. I'm both fascinated by and dismayed that beyond two years old, we must all of a sudden "get with the program," and are given messages like "C'mon, be a big girl now," or "There's no reason to cry." We start suppressing our fragile, vulnerable selves and bury them underground. The pain doesn't go away, and as a result, we self-numb. When a client has shared some way they sabotaged themselves, there's usually something that triggered it. It's often a wound that's not being addressed and instead of self-soothing, they're self-numbing so they can "get over it."

There's so much more to say about this, but to start your own inquiry, I suggest you look at ways to self-soothe. This is more about rebuilding and re-parenting than about energizing and re-booting your mojo.

Reflection Check-In

Tuning In versus Zoning Out

* What is a challenge that you're dealing with right now that is putting you on Dimmers (e.g., egregious boss who's continually snarky to me)?

* How does it impact you (e.g., I start feeling like I'm doomed and nothing I can do is right)?

* What is a constructive action that you can take to address it (e.g., watch SMART SEXY TV episode on "How to Un-Stress in Five Minutes or Less" so when I'm triggered I don't get reactive and can reboot)?

* What would be a Tuning-In action that could nurture your spirit and help you reboot (e.g., spend time with a fun friend who makes me laugh and reinforces how smart and competent I really am)?

Here are a few examples that I suggest and have used:

* **Journaling**—Dialogue with the part of you that's in pain and the loving parent within. Scream on the page and don't be a "good girl" or "good boy." Let it rip. Nobody died from you venting your upset on the page, but be discreet about where you leave your journal and make sure nobody has access to it.

* **Goddess Vent**—Call a friend and say, "Hey, I am really hurting and just need someone to listen to me. Be VERY intentional about who you call and look at exactly what you need. As I've mentioned before, people who are problem solvers and fixers by nature are terrific when you need a strategy but can be totally counter-productive when you're in pain.

* **Connect with your sensuality**—I find that when we connect with some form of our sensuality, we're reminded that we are NOT just our hurts but a complete holistic being. Some examples can be a very hot salt bath with lavender, a yoga class, moving to evocative music, making art, intense aerobic activity, watching a film that is thematic with what you're going through, or walking in nature.

✳ **Take an action that reflects your most alive state**— Many people share that even taking fifteen minutes to re- organize something in their life makes them feel more in control and less at the mercy of their circumstances. There are also programs available on the internet that assist people in how to self-soothe that I list on the resources page at the back of the book.

✳ **Let yourself feel what you feel**—Give yourself permis- sion to feel what you feel. Express what you need to ex- press in appropriate way to others. The more emotionally fluid you become the quicker you'll reconnect with your vitality. Kids are our greatest teachers in this area—they cry one moment and are laughing the next.

These are my suggestions; what are some of yours?

Reflection Check-In: Self-Soothing vs. Self-Numbing

✳ One source of pain or upset in your life is (e.g., I'm in between jobs and am very scared about what the next chapter looks like for me):

✳ The feelings or negative self-talk you experience as a result are (e.g., if I had done my job right I never would have been downsized, I messed up yet again!):

✳ What is the most effective way that you can self-soothe right now (e.g., set up a coffee date twice a month with people who may have contacts and have offered to help me, write an Evidence List to remind myself how accomplished and resilient I really am, and read it every morning)?

Girls Just Want to Have Fun

In honor of my anthem, Cyndy Lauper's song, "Girls Just Want to Have Fun," I encourage you, my Fab Fierce Ones, to create your own "Girls Just Want to Have Fun" List, that you can refer to, tweak, cross off, accomplish, and just plain enjoy.

My "Girls Just Want to Have Fun" List is as follows:

* Architecture Tours.
* Thrift Shopping.
* Going dancing.
* Girls night out doing anything.
* Indoor spa night.
* Listening to music that's really upbeat.
* Clothing swap.
* High tea with a bunch of Audacious Girls wearing gloves and hats.
* Getting lost in bookstores (whichever ones still remain).

I've given you a whole slew of tools and exercises to move from Dimmers to Shimmers on a moment-to-moment basis. Some you'll connect with more than others. Make them your own and see it as a creative process. When we harness and focus our vitality and joy, we not only elevate our own happiness but those around us. When we stay focused on our natural inextinguishable light, we take a bodacious step toward having the Courage to SPARKLE.

EXERCISES

✳ ✳ ✳ ✳

Exercise 1—Envy to EN-SPIRATION

You find out one of your colleagues has a prestigious position where she's meeting very influential people doing what she loves.

* ✳ You are envious of (e.g., Susan's job): _____.

* ✳ You are envious because (e.g., her career is very exciting and I feel really stuck in mine): _____.

* ✳ If you were to get EN-SPIRED by what he/she/they have, you would (e.g., spend more time creating important relationships, build my confidence, take more risks, be willing to ask for help, and not worry so much if I was ready but rather just jump in and go for it): _____.

* ✳ What are the core values you want more of in your life (e.g., trust, adventure, confidence, prestige, and financial success)?

* ✳ What can you learn from the person you're envying (e.g., to stay focused on what I really want and to have the confidence to go for it)?

* ✳ What small or big action will you take to get EN-SPIRED (e.g., look at what new position I'd like to aspire to in my company and join a committee where I can meet influential people)?

The more we get EN-SPIRED by those who trigger our envy, the more we'll stay on track in our own lives.

Exercise 2—Self-Care/Morning Ritual

* What part of the section on Self-Care speaks to you the most?

* If you had to name the top three to four areas of your Self-Care, what would they be?

* What is a fun name to give your Self-Care?

* What is the best, most engaging way to track and monitor your Self-Care?

* What is a small action you can take in each area?

* How can you include an action into your morning ritual?

* What will be a way to celebrate having taken those actions?

Exercise 3—Work-Life Integration

* What did you take away from the Work-Life Integration section in this Gem?

* How can you apply it to your life?

* What is a small but consistent action you can take?

* When will you take it?

* What do you hope to accomplish by taking it?

* How can you celebrate having taken it?

Exercise 4—Energy Drainers/Energy Gainers

Make a list of your Energy Drainers and Energy Gainers. Once you fill out the list, ask yourself these questions:

* What is one Energy Drainer I will eliminate this week (e.g., I hate commuting via public transportation, so I will

speak to my boss about the possibility of coming in an hour earlier so I can drive in instead)?

* What is one Energy Gainer that I'll add to my week (e.g., I love gardening and will take an extra fifteen minutes to putter in it, before having to catch up on e-mails)?

Check-In

* What did you learn from this Gem?
* How will you apply it to your life?
* What is one small or big action you will take right now?

GEM 10

✳ ✳ ✳ ✳

CREATING YOUR SCINTILLATING CIRCLE OF SUPPORT

Clarifying What You Need from Your Team

Some of us may live on an island, but we're not an island. We must have community and support in our lives in order to SPARKLE. Having a circle of support allows us to shine and show up in the world with our most alive selves. We also get to do that for others. Life becomes less of a grind, more of a journey of discovery, adventure and growth. We are better able to deal with pain in life and more able to celebrate the joys when we surround ourselves with our tribe, Our Possibility Posse, our Team SPARKLE. As you're defining and refining what your Team SPARKLE looks like, it's vital to look at what you need from your team. Here's a list of what I need from my team that spans both my personal and professional aspirations and dreams.

I need people on my team to:

✳ Have fun with.

✳ Learn from and grow with.

✳ Share the narrative of my life with.

✳ Offer rapt attention.

✳ Tell me the truth in a kind and compassionate way.

* Make me laugh so hard that I have tears streaming down my face.

* Have adventures with.

* Guide me in the right direction when I need greater clarity.

* Celebrate my victories.

* Pick me up when I've fallen down.

* Let me say "Ouch!" when I'm hurting without trying to fix my pain or tell me something that sucks doesn't suck.

* Remind me to slow down.

* Tell me to "put on my big girl pants" and do it anyway even though I'm scared.

* ... and not be too hard on myself when I'm being too hard on myself.

* Brainstorm with.

* Expand my world by connecting me with people, places, and ideas.

* Drink in the wonder of art and nature.

* Remind me to trust myself and the process.

* Point me to my blind spots.

* Mourn the heartbreak as well as celebrate the gorgeous parts of being alive.

* Keep my dreams alive even though sometimes they may feel way too off in the distance, and...

* Remind me that they are all possible in due time.

It is one of my greatest joys in life to *do the same* for them in my own way. It's clearly a very long and mighty list; some might say it's a tall order. I know that it's totally possible. I see the miracle of having a Team SPARKLE in my own and others' lives. Some of what's on my list will inspire you, remind you, and reinforce what you already have or want to create. It's your list and your Team SPARKLE.

Checking-In—What Do You Need from Your Team SPARKLE?

Take a moment right now and close your eyes. If you want, you can put on some music that will evoke the feelings of community and connection, or daydream about what you need from your Team SPARKLE.

When you're ready, take out your C2S Workbook (colored pencils and markers are helpful as well) and answer the following question:

* What do you need from your community, right now?
* What does it *look* like?
* What does it *feel* like?
* Anything else?
* Feel free to draw images as well.
* What do you provide for your community?
* What do you want to provide for your Team SPARKLE?

In addition to looking at what you'd like your Team SPARKLE to provide for you, it's equally important to look at what you enjoy providing for them. By doing so, you can do it with an open heart and a spirit of generosity, which of course puts you on Shimmers but also connects you with your community.

Two of my dear friends and long-time clients are Tali and Ophi Edut, aka The Astro Twins. They are identical twins that are savvy, super smart astrologers and yet they provide so much more than astrology to their community. No matter where we go, in whatever social situations they're in, everyone is captivated by them.

It becomes abundantly clear why they are so successful in their business. In sharing their knowledge of astrology, they provide the gifts of perspective, encouragement, and entertainment to their community. They elegantly co-mingle their love of astrology with their passion for helping people to feel inspired and empowered. Someone will often come to them frustrated by a partner who's being a real PITA (pain in the ass) and that same person will walk away with sound advice on how to navigate the rough edges of life and feel a palpable relief. Ophi and Tali are always light-hearted in their delivery, avoiding the peril of taking themselves too seriously that is so endemic in Personal Growth and many New Age modalities.

I often ask my clients what people come to them for, perhaps it's for advice, a sounding board, or to help them lighten up. I also ask my clients to share a time that helping someone in their life felt really rewarding. By identifying when you feel inspired by having provided something to someone in your life bring us back to what makes us SPARKLE, what I spoke about in Gem 1—Mining for Your SPARKLE. When we look at the *Doing* and *Being* part of our life purpose, we can start to see how it seamlessly intersects with what we already enjoy providing for our community.

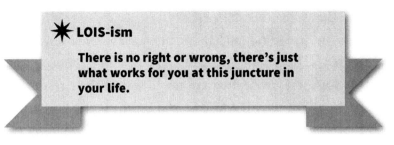

✳ LOIS-ism

There is no right or wrong, there's just what works for you at this juncture in your life.

REFLECTION CHECK-IN

✳ What do you want to provide for your team and in your community?

✳ What do people come to you for?

✳ What are those things you enjoy?

✳ Anything else?

✳ Feel free to draw images as well.

Consider where you're at in your life at this moment when you look at both what you need from your Team SPARKLE, and what you are willing to provide. At different times, you'll need different things in addition to being able to provide different things at different times. Being certain about what you can and can't provide is of utmost importance. It allows you to cut yourself some slack while still being there for others.

Knowing What You Don't Want to or Can't Provide for Your Community

It's equally important to know what you *do not* want to provide for your community. If you don't want to do something, even if you're good at it, don't do it. You'll feel resentful and it won't serve anyone.

One example of this shows up in a specific area of my career coaching work. Helping my clients think through the clarification and research process of what is next for them career-wise, in addition to helping them to nail their interviews is something I am both skilled at and passionate about. During that process, they will often ask me to review their resumes. I enjoy wordsmithing, identifying the more compelling use of language, and helping them to specify their unique skill set and offerings. However, when it comes to doing an overhaul of their resume, I refer it out. I don't enjoy it and I know I won't provide the most value compared to someone who does that as their specialty. We need to pay as much attention to what we don't want to provide for our community as what we do want to.

Granted, there are times that doing something for a friend or business acquaintance is inconvenient but we do it anyway. We may want to be helpful and generous or because it serves us in some way, that's not what I'm talking about here. I'm speaking of the perils of chronic people-pleasing or as I call it "people-displeasing." When we are not being honest, and keep doing things that we are resentful of doing, nobody wins because we're not doing your best work and it shows. It can strain your relationships. However, when you know what you do and don't want to provide for your community, and honor it to the best of your ability, you will put both yourself and those you serve, in a position to SPARKLE.

Take a moment to look in your own life and ask yourself what might you need to let go of providing for others, right now.

REFLECTION CHECK-IN

* ✴ Given where you are right now in my life, you can provide: _____ .

* ✴ You cannot provide: _____ .

Make Sure Your Community is In-Line with Your Values and Goals

When women come to me for help attracting their life partner, one of the first things I ask is who in their lives are role models in terms of partnerships or marriages that they look up to. Many respond that they are either surrounded by people whose relationships look like a train wreck, or by what I call the "Wall of Women," which is a plethora of unmarried and un-partnered women. One of the first things I suggest is for them to actively pursue having couples in their lives who they admire and can learn from their partnerships. We must surround ourselves with a community that both mirrors and supports our values and our goals.

For example, if you want to be an entrepreneur but everyone in your circle works for a steady paycheck and places stability over freedom, chances are, you're not going to get the necessary support you need. They can be there for you in a myriad of other ways. You will need to actively recruit people into your life that are aligned with your expanded vision of your desired entrepreneurial yearnings.

> **✴ LOIS-ism**
>
> **Don't ask someone to be who they're not. Ask yourself *if* and *how* they fit into your life.**

"Expectations are planned disappointments." I love that aphorism. When we expect people to be someone they're not, or provide what they can't, we stop appreciating them for who they are and what they *can* provide. No matter how much you love or care about someone, there will invariably be a time where they fall short of your expectations or hurt your feelings. It's a guaranteed because we're human—one of the things that clients and friends struggle with when that happens.

As I mentioned previously, there are times in our lives where *we* may not have it in us to give and neither do other people. They may float in and out of our circle of friends. Sometimes, we're closer to them than other times. Perhaps there's an innocent misunderstanding and a simple non-defensive conversation can clean it up. Other times, it doesn't make sense to have the conversation because you have to chalk it up to "that's just the way they are," and accept them as they are. There's a huge freedom in doing that. Nothing is more exhausting than asking a person to be someone they're not. They feel resentful and you feel frustrated. It simply doesn't work.

When we can accept where people are at, we are freed up to let go of expectations and appreciate them for who they are while understanding who they are not.

A-B-C Circle of Connection

This is where using a principle I call, The A-B-C Circle of Connection, is useful. Your "A" circle is the one filled with your "family of choice," (which could easily include your family of origin as well) the people you know have got your back, and you've got theirs'. They're the "A-List" of your personal celebrities, your posse. The "B" circle is more like your entourage: great for a good time and emotional support, but you just don't feel quite as close to them as your "A" circle. You are still there for them and they are there for you in both the celebration and setbacks of life. The "C" circle is your acquaintances and good-times buddies, folks you call with extra concert tickets or to catch up with over drinks or coffee now and then.

One client came to me distraught that whenever her BFF, clearly "A" circle, started seeing a new man, she felt ignored and brushed to the side. When the relationship crashed and burned, my client would jump in and save the day. They would soon return to their BFF status, but then it would happen again. Clearly, it was an upsetting experience for my client, who felt unappreciated and used. She would have these "crash and burn/save the day" conversations about it with her friend but the pattern kept repeating. It was her friend's blind spot. In so many ways, she was really a terrific friend but this particular dynamic made my client sad, resentful and, at the time, wanting to write her off.

I strongly suggested that she not do that but instead I encouraged her to *energetically move her friend to an outer circle* when she was in "man at the center of her universe" mode. My client looked at me rather confused. How could she keep going back and forth in how she held her friendship? I asked her to consider that if her girlfriend during her "guy vacuum time" was more like a "B" or "C" circle friend, would she feel so distraught about this scenario? Would she feel the need to jump in and save the day? She said, "Absolutely not. I'd just give her some space and put my focus into my closer friendships. I certainly wouldn't be there, however, to pick up the pieces."

Knowing that her friend went into the hormonal haze of a romance trance with a new boyfriend, my client started making the adjustment. Taking that approach also gave her perspective to look at her own issues about being single as well. On a practical level, the first thing she did was to give her BFF a lot of slack during the first two to three months of her relationships, knowing how the early stages of infatuation are often intense. She knew she wouldn't be a top priority and with that realization, she didn't set herself up for being disappointed. Her friend was grateful for being given the space she needed. While my client missed the old connection, she was able to refocus her energy and time on other relationships in her life as well as on her own goals.

The success of this practice is based on the ability to make these choices with full awareness and compassion for both yourself and the other person. This is not about punishing people by "demoting" them. Rather, it's a re-adjusting of our expectations, granting people the space to be where they are at, and still find a level of connection that works for us with key people in our lives.

I've had moments in my own life where I considered a friend to be in my "A" circle but their actions kept showing me that they didn't see me the same way. Instead of being a Drama Queen about it, I moved them to a "B" or "C" circle, dropping my own expectations considerably in the process. We got along great.

REFLECTION CHECK-IN

* Take a moment to take out your C2S Workbook and draw three circles.

* Label each circle A, B, and C, and put different people's names in each circle that signify your current level of connection.

✳ Circle "A"—Inner Circle people whom you're *very* close to.

✳ Circle "B"—Close friends whom you enjoy being with but are not your Inner Circle.

✳ Circle "C"—People you may socialize with once in a while that you enjoy but you're not that close with.

BONUS

✳ Given what you're up to in your life who in your circles, might need additional attention? Which ones might require additional boundaries? What topics do you need to eliminate with others in your circles?

✳ Start to think about your different circles and how this exercise can support you in building your Team SPARKLE.

Finding Community at Work

This concept was covered in more depth in Gem 8—How to Shine in your Career, but a few words about it here won't hurt. Work is a huge part of our lives, and where we make many of the friends who later become intimate parts of our "A" or "B" circles. If we move to a new city, it can be the first place we look for new friends. It's important to also look for a compatible work culture where finding those friends is a real possibility. Individual departments and teams within the larger company have different subcultures, and that may be enough for you to thrive in. If you don't like any of the people you work with, it's probably time to find a new job.

In cases where you work for yourself and are a team of one, it's equally important to determine your desired culture. Some of my clients, who are solo-preneurs, know they must be around other people or they feel isolated and in a vacuum. Folks like this often end up renting shared workspaces or working in cafes just for the human company. Others need more solitary time, and that's one reason why they're working for themselves.

The take-away here is to know how you work, and what kind of culture allows you to do your best work.

REFLECTION CHECK-IN

* What type of friendships are important for you to cultivate at work?
* What would Team SPARKLE look like for you at work?
* What small action can you take to build a few important relationships at work?

Creating Deep and Meaningful Relationships in Your Life

Whether you're an introvert, extrovert, or something in between chances are the richness and connection of our relationships deeply impacts our sense of fulfillment in our life and our ability to SPARKLE. When all the toys and "stuff" that we thought mattered falls away, we start to see that the bonds we have with each other are of the deepest meaning to us. We need each other.

Find a Circle of Loving and Compassionate Truth Tellers

This is my bias and I'm waving my banner proudly. Nothing, and I mean *nothing*, will make you heal and grow more, than surrounding yourself with compassionate truth tellers. The real deal about the Courage to SPARKLE is that while it's a wonderful goal to shine brightly and share your gifts freely and feel fulfilled, it can also be very confrontational for ourselves and others. We come up against all the resistance that stopped us in the first place. We just do. Not because we're doing anything wrong, but because if it was that easy to be doing it, we'd be doing it all the time, so would everyone else.

When you make an active choice to surround yourself with people you trust, who will tell you the truth from a compassionate place, your life will never be the same. You'll start to fall in love with the truth, and it will set you free; though it will piss you off in the meantime!

Here's an example: I'm a Recovering Good Girl and Chronic People Pleaser. Nothing killed my spirit more than pretending to be someone I wasn't to the point that I didn't know who I was anymore. I felt like an imposter in my own life. Conversely, surrounding myself with people who are willing to be honest with me, but in a kind and compassionate way, has allowed me to grow exponentially. As a result, I've learned how to develop a thick skin while still being quite sensitive. I'm less daunted by transparency than I used to be, and I am more able to "out" myself in terms of when I'm doing things that don't serve me or are outright self-sabotaging. Instead of being slammed and judged for it, my friends and I will usually laugh, because they too, recognize themselves in my "embarrassing self-disclosure."

One thing I've noticed about truly successful people—and what I mean by successful is not *only* financially successful, but those who are truly happy—is they don't seek out a lot of "yes" people around them. They often have people in their lives "who knew them when." We need to surround ourselves with people we trust will tell us the truth so we won't be "yes-ed" or Polyanna-ed over (yes, I just turned Pollyanna into a verb). Do yourself a favor and actively seek out compassionate truth tellers who want the same compassionate honesty from you. Chances are, you'll have a friend for life.

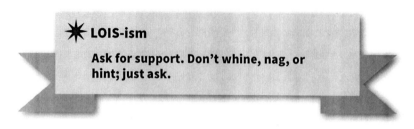

✳ LOIS-ism

Ask for support. Don't whine, nag, or hint; just ask.

I am still amazed how hard it is to ask for support. When I was writing this book, I was concerned that I would feel like I was in a vacuum. Despite my Itty Bitty Committee that yammered endlessly that I was "bothering" people, I asked people I loved, trusted, if they'd be willing to give me honest feedback on my book. I breathed hard and hit "Send" to my email outreach. To my delight, I received a full-frontal blast of a "feeling the love" response. Even those who said they wouldn't be able to read my book shared that they were overjoyed that I was writing a book. So many people offered to help in one way or another. While I knew there would be a considerable drop-off (there usually is) I ended up with a small but mighty core of people who did give me very useful and supportive feedback. I didn't feel like I had to lean heavily on any one or two people. Every time I sat down to the computer to write, I thought of them. Some people were dippers that would read a chapter or two and say "keep going." Others were divers that gave me incredibly detailed feedback on what was and wasn't working. My experience of writing this book got transformed by doing it in a community.

As women, we often have a hard time asking for support. Instead of being direct and succinct, we go the roundabout way because being direct brings up a lot of issues for us. As a result, we do the following: apologize, over-explain, bargain, whine, presume, feel entitled, or hint. The more skilled and specific we are with asking for help and offering support to others, the more we'll experience the joy of being in community. Practice makes progress. Remember how good it feels to make a difference for others? Well, it's the same when others can do that for us!

Team SPARKLE Success (versus Cheat) Sheet

When we think of our Scintillating Circle of Support, aka Team SPARKLE, it's really important to remember the following things:

* Relationships shift and change. The more we accept that, the more we'll enjoy the process.

* Be clear about what you need from your community and what you want to provide.

* Be realistic about what you can and can't provide, and have the same acceptance for those in your circle.

* Cherish and celebrate what they can do.

* Acknowledge, acknowledge, acknowledge. There's just not enough *please* and *thank you* in the world. When we acknowledge those around us, we're reminded how blessed we are, and they experience satisfaction knowing they made a difference for you.

* Give people the space to be amazing and they will be.

Check-In

* What did you learn about your Team SPARKLE from this Gem?

* How does it apply to your life right now?

* What small action can you take right now?

GEM 11

✴   ✴   ✴   ✴

COMMUNICATION THAT GLISTENS

In Gem 9—From Dimmers to Shimmers, I spoke about how the little things in life that we don't address quickly become the big things. When we communicate with a spirit of generosity and goodwill, the little things have less opportunity to become the big things. In doing so, we deepen our connections with others, experience the true gifts that our community provides, and are freed to show up in the world in a vibrant way. We can SPARKLE.

The Power of Feedback

Effectively given feedback is one of the most important elements in building confidence, learning and growing, and deepening intimacy and connections with others. The clearer you are about the type of feedback you are looking for and the more open you remain to receiving it, the greater the chance that you'll reap the benefits.

Honoring Your Own Edges

An author, who was a pioneer in the area of women's psychology, was well aware that the book she was working on was provocative and would probably get a fair amount of pushback. She also knew that she had to write it despite the potentially mixed reviews. She was a truth-teller, a visionary, but also vulnerable. She needed both support to keep going through what would be a long and arduous process, plus she needed the courage—the Courage to SPARKLE.

On a fairly consistent basis while writing her book, she'd invite her Inner Circle into her home and read a section of the book aloud. During the first several meetings, the only feedback she wanted was encouragement and lots of "you can do it!" While fierce in her commitment, she knew she was too sensitive to receive even the slightest albeit constructive criticism.

With every feedback session and as she continued her work, she gained confidence about the importance of her message and the value it would provide to women. In time, she was able to ask for a wider range of feedback. By the last meeting, she had built up her confidence enough that she was freely able to ask her Inner Circle to be 100% candid. She integrated the feedback, along with the insights she had gleaned along the way, into both the book itself and the book proposal.

Several hundreds of rejection slips later, she sold the book and it became a bestseller. Ironically, she opted to wallpaper her bathroom with the publication rejection letters (it was the pre-digital age of course) to remind herself that "they," meaning the powers that be, aren't always right and to keep going no matter what. I love this story so much because it teaches us the power of learning how to ask for what we need and nurture ourselves in a way that makes a difference in our own life. In doing so, we're that much more able to contribute to the world around us.

A Few Tips for Asking for Feedback

* Be specific about the type of feedback you're looking for.

* Make sure that the person you're asking is able to provide it to you. Don't ask someone to provide something for you that they are unable to give, as discussed in Gem 10— Creating Your Scintillating Circle of Support.

* Ask for further clarification if you are not sure exactly what the person is trying to communicate. Don't make assumptions.

* Do your best to remain open to it.

* Thank them for giving it to you even if you may not agree with everything they say.

* Breathe.

* Sort out what doesn't feel relevant and what does, even if it makes you uncomfortable.

A Few Tips for Providing Feedback

* Ask if they would like feedback. Such a simple yet profound thing, sometimes people actually appear to want feedback but they actually just need to feel heard.

* Ask what type of feedback would be most useful. Doing this allows people to clarify for themselves what type of input would be most valuable.

* Find a way to say it in a very clear and succinct manner.

* Check in to see if the person understands it and make sure they reflect it back for the sake of clarity.

* Even if the feedback is something that may be uncomfortable for them to hear, offer it in the spirit of wanting to support or contribute to them.

Feedback ultimately is a lot like the Golden Rule: give unto others as you would have them give unto you.

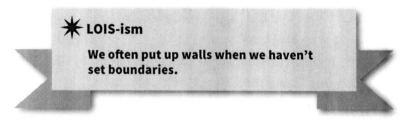

LOIS-ism

We often put up walls when we haven't set boundaries.

The Power of Boundaries

Having boundaries is also an essential communication tool for building meaningful relationships, both personal and professionally. If we have no boundaries or they are too porous, it becomes the breeding ground for resentment and assumptions. Boundaries are often seen as a way to keep people at bay or at a distance, but well-established boundaries stated in a clear and succinct manner, actually do the opposite. Each of you knows where the other stands, plain and simple. A simple boundary, clearly stated and honored, solidifies and deepens relationships. As women, the more we set boundaries in simple and concise ways, and from a place of worthiness, the more empowered we'll feel. The more ability we'll have to show up as our best selves and support others to do the same.

So many breakdowns in communication happen because we don't set boundaries clearly or clarify ones that seem rather tenuous. For example, one of my clients felt like she "had to" work later hours even though she had never clarified her exact hours with her boss. She made a lot of assumptions about what time she "should" leave instead of actually having a conversation about it. She was exhausted by the end of the day, which was definitely not her most productive time, and was resentful.

After a few sessions and some role-plays, she began to see that so many of her actions were based on assumptions. They were rooted in old beliefs about needing to be "nice" and "compliant" rather than direct in her communication. When she did have the conversation with her boss about wanting to leave at a certain hour, he looked at her, perplexed. He said, "You're a grown-up, you do your work. Leave when you want. Everyone else does." She was relieved and dismayed that this simple issue was illegally subletting her gray matter, when in fact, a simple conversation that took about five minutes, cleared it up. My client, by the way, is in a senior level position with a sterling reputation. You can see that this issue affects women at all ages and stages of their life.

> ✳ **LOIS-ism**
>
> **Setting boundaries is a lot easier than resetting boundaries.**

As I mentioned in Gem 8, where I discussed culture shopping, some work cultures have covert (and egregious) forms of communication that are toxic, but most are not that way. If you simply set a boundary or inquire about an unclear one, it can dissipate a lot of stress.

If you're not used to setting boundaries, it can feel really confronting and you may want to gloss over it and avoid doing it. I can guarantee you it is much harder to re-set a boundary than to set it right at the beginning. People get in a groove and don't always adapt to changing up the rules. All you have to do is see what happens when the mom who has been a "one-stop shop for everyone else's needs" starts setting boundaries and saying "no," to being everything to everyone. The troops get really cranky.

Even when you set boundaries, there will always be times when both parties slip back and let boundaries slide. When that happens, just reset them. If you're able to, it's best if you make it about "getting back on track" versus getting into a power struggle. When boundaries are continuously not being honored or you're not honoring someone else's, look at where the challenge might be. Maybe the boundary needs to be tweaked a bit, or during a particular deadline you have to be a little looser. That's fine, but make sure to communicate about it.

Of course, there are those people who are largely "allergic" to boundaries. Card-carrying narcissists usually hate boundaries because it insinuates that another independent planet exists in what they assumed was "their own private solar system." Only you can decide what makes sense in terms of how much contact you need or must have with that type of person, or the conversations that need to be had. If someone consistently dishonors your boundary, you may want to look at how much involvement you want with them.

Anger is usually a sign that our boundaries have either not been set or honored, and it can be a very instructive emotion as long as we process it properly. Like the difference between crude oil, which comes out of the ground like a thick mud, versus petroleum that's been processed for you to put in your tank to get you moving, processing our anger is equally effective. Try putting crude oil in your tank and see how far it will get you—about as far as blasting someone with the full bounty of your anger! It is much better to figure out where it's coming from first, and address that issue instead.

Reality Check—When Trusting Yourself is Knowing when Not to Trust Yourself

You will hear me talk a lot about the importance for women to learn how to "trust ourselves" because it's one of the major things that prevents us from shining brightly in the world. A key part of trusting ourselves is knowing when we can't trust ourselves. If I go to the grocery store when I'm hungry, I have a far better chance of ending up with a cartload of carbs and maybe a head of kale (if I'm lucky). If I take the time, however, to eat a good meal, have a grocery list of healthy foods, maybe one single treat, I'm guaranteed to make better choices.

Whether it's personal or professional, when we see we are reactive or are not clear about the next right step to take, it's always helpful to get a reality check about our opinions, thoughts, or behaviors. In addition to asking a trusted friend or colleague, you can also choose to put your decision on hold, sleep on it, journal about it, or get well informed feedback before making your decision. It's a lot easier to avoid a fire rather than to have to put one out.

Dealing with the Big "C": Conflict

I was intrigued to learn this was true. What a rich metaphor for relationships that once had some strain or broken places in them and are now stronger as the result of effective communication. When it comes to communication skills and emotional intelligence, some people have a triple-decker, steamer-sized tool chest. Other people have a toy toolbox with just a plastic hammer and nail. I'm someone who still resists having the difficult conversations. Yet in most cases, I find when

> ✳ **LOIS-ism**
>
> **Broken bones that heal properly
> become stronger than bones that were
> never broken in the first place.**

I start them with an intention to grow, to heal the relationship, and to learn about both myself and the other person in the process, I come away deeply relieved and feel more connected to them. I'll probably never jump and shout with joy declaring, "Oh, goodie! I get to have a challenging conversation in service of strengthening my communication skills and creating a win-win situation." I have witnessed, over and over, that when I follow a few key principles and strategies, it makes all the difference in the world. Here are some suggestions to get you started.

Honor Your Triggers—Most of the time, when we have a strong reaction to what someone else says and does, it comes from a historical pattern of something that happened at an early age that we may or may not be aware of. I have seen the sheer act of taking a moment to pause, breathe, and identify the message you feel you are getting (e.g., "nobody ever listens to me," "it's always my fault," and so on) start increasing awareness that allows us to move forward on what I call the "Course Correction" track. I go into greater detail on that in Gem 12. The more aware you become of your core messages and triggers, the better the chances are that you'll become less reactive and more proactive when speaking with anyone. You get to own your stuff. There's a huge power in that, and the more you can do that, the better the chance you'll have a positive outcome if/when you decide to have the conversation.

Goddess Vent—I have mentioned the Goddess Vent before and I'm a huge fan of it. I have several women in my life who have gifted me with the privilege of Goddess Venting. In short, it's calling someone you really trust and asking for a time to express why you're upset at a situation. You're asking for their rapt attention and listening ear, but not necessarily for advice. Often, just feeling heard will shift your mood. Make sure to let the person know that all you need to do is share. Nothing is more annoying than getting feedback when you're not ready to hear it when you simply need a kind, listening ear.

I'm not talking about whining for hours and holding people captive while you drown in a sea of self-pity. All you need sometimes is ten or fifteen minutes of their time to let it rip. Let yourself get messy, fire your Inner Nancy Nice-y. Don't worry; you'll regain your composure once you feel more heard.

Save as Draft—If you can't find someone to speak to or you're not the Goddess Vent type person, write out everything you'd like to say, no holds barred. Let it rip and then DO NOT SEND. I repeat: DO NOT SEND. *Save as Draft* has saved many a butt. Once you have had some time to "sleep on it," you'll be really relieved that you didn't send it. You'll be able to gain perspective and tease out what you do and don't want to say. Don't get nailed via e-mail after saying something you later regret.

Be in Their World—The more we can understand what another person is going through the more compassionate we can be with them. This is not about condoning unacceptable behavior but rather having a perspective of what another person's experience is. One of my most powerful lessons in this area, was when I was a volunteer who lead a reading group for a sixth-grade class. This little girl kept disrupting the session by hanging off her chair, playing with my long hair, and trying to sit on my lap. Clearly, she was desperate for attention. As I was about to lose patience with her and reprimand her, another student who was reading out loud, stumbled on a word and asked 'What does it mean when someone is bald?' The little girl who was making all the commotion called out, "It means your mom's in chemotherapy." I'll never forget that moment. I was reminded how quickly our perspective changes when we realize what's going on in another person's life.

Focus on Your Desired Outcome—When we're just reactive, it's easy to focus on being right; it's all too human. When we can take a step back and ask ourselves, "What's the desired outcome?" we may have a very different approach and, response. The clearer you are about what goal or outcome you'd like, the clearer you'll be on the best approach to get there.

When you stub your toe or run into a wall, you say "Ouch!" The release of sound and giving voice to the pain is enormously freeing. Admitting when we're in pain can be very therapeutic, rather than feeling like we have to soldier on unacknowledged. The sheer expression is restorative. We can move on. Try it the next time you feel in emotional pain. Let out a giant, "OUCH!" freely and boldly with no apology. It's a lot more effective behind closed doors so you don't have to censor yourself.

Avoid TYM and Other Ways We Kill Intimacy

No matter how old we are, when we get our feelings hurt or are disappointed, it's easy to go into what I call "taking your marbles" (TYM) and going home. You shut down, you self-protect, you start building a case against the person who's hurt you. You write them off and retreat. It makes sense. When we get our feelings hurt or deal with pain, it brings us back to a wounded part of us, often from childhood. We didn't have the words or ability to express ourselves then. Few of us were taught past a certain age that expressing upset is human. We all do it. The difference is how quickly we can rebound and clean it up.

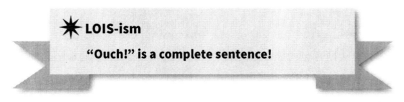

★ LOIS-ism

"Ouch!" is a complete sentence!

Recently, I did my own TYM with a man I'm dating. It was our second date and we went to a movie. I winced and squirmed in a scene where, out of nowhere, a character pulled a gun. My date said out loud, "Oh come on!" Truth be told, I did a total TYM. My "stop being so sensitive button" had been pressed and I felt my heart shut down.

After the movie, I watched myself being cordial but distant. I saw the potential spiraling down of what started out as a fun and playful date, into a strained one due to my going into TYM mode. I repeated my mantra, "Do I want to be right, or do I want to have an enjoyable evening?" Luckily, I opted for the latter. I let him know in an appropriate way that I felt hurt by his "Oh come on!" I shared that it stung because I felt like I was being reprimanded for being too emotional. It turned out he was reacting to his own irritation with the movie because he found the scene totally unbelievable. He added that he's fine with however I react to movies. I was so glad that I opted to say something instead of staying in my TYM territory. I see this TYM behavior in so many situations, and it really breaks my heart to see people stuck in old counter-productive patterns of strained communication based on early behavioral triggers.

A spiritual mentor of mine handled his rambunctious teenage son with tremendous skill and patience. His wife stood slack-jawed and quizzed him on how he could stay so cool and together while having what could easily be a really volatile dialogue. My mentor responded to her, "I can do that because I spend as much time monitoring my own reactions as I do our son's. As a result, I know when to say something, and more important, when to be quiet." More and more, I see that urgency or a need to get the last word in, or impulsivity, has less to do with addressing the real-timeliness of the issue and more about not being able to tolerate our own anxiety.

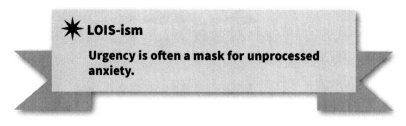

✷ LOIS-ism

Urgency is often a mask for unprocessed anxiety.

The Three Glittering Phrases That Transform Difficult Conversations

When dealing with a difficult conversation, I find having scripts with a few bullet points to be very helpful. Even having a few well-turned phrases can allow you to feel more confident and conversational.

Most of the time, when we're upset at what someone did or said we resort to:

Punishing them.

Making them guess why we're angry at them.

Pretending nothing is wrong.

OR

We can use one of these three glittering phrases to create an open dialogue and bring some compassion to what can be an otherwise very uncomfortable and potentially defensive conversation.

* **I'm confused**—Excellent when someone is giving you mixed messages that you want to clarify.

* **I'm fascinated**—When somebody's behavior doesn't make sense. Who doesn't like it when others feel "fascinated" by something we did or said? It changes the tone from combative to potentially interesting and thought-provoking.

* **I'm curious**—When you are genuinely curious and want to understand another person's action and behavior. It de-escalates what can be a potentially volatile situation.

Humor is one of the greatest resources we have to resolve conflict. The more we can laugh at ourselves and the situation, the more we can skillfully resolve life's conflicts. Recently, I had a communication glitch with a potential speaking client. I certainly didn't want to lose the client or start off on a bad foot, but I also didn't want to get into a long she said/she said conversation. I simply texted her, "Clearly a misunderstanding, let's tawk!"

As soon as she got on the phone, I decided to approach her very playfully and said, "Remember that party game we played as a little kid called 'telephone'?" (The game where one person whispers a phrase in another person's ear and it goes down the line from there, and what the last person says is totally different than the initial message.) She knew full well where I was going with it. "I think we're playing it right now, without realizing it!" We both laughed, and moved on with the conversation with a positive outcome.

> ✳ **LOIS-ism**
>
> **Humor is the sorbet of the soul.**
> **It clears life's palette of many challenges.**

Acknowledge, Acknowledge, Acknowledge

There are several phrases and philosophies that deserve repetition in learning to communicate. Most of learning is being reminded, and then integrating what we are reminded of into our lives. I can't say enough about the power of acknowledging people in our lives, all aspects of our lives. We can't get enough of being acknowledged for our gifts, our good qualities, and the difference we make in the world. I'm not talking about gushing, or being disingenuous. Of course, what's most important is that our behaviors match our words of praise; that being said, we come alive when we are appreciated and valued.

Sunflowers are one of my favorite flowers. They are big, bold, and always seem like they're smiling. They make me happy looking at them. I see praise and acknowledgment in the same roles as the sun, water, and fertile soil, making us burst forth as proudly and boldly as my dear friend the sunflower.

Acknowledgment comes very naturally to me. I derive enormous joy watching people light up as I give it so I don't have to think about it much. I do suggest to my clients that they acknowledge, compliment, or thank three people a day. You'll be delighted to see how this small act impacts us and them so profoundly. They smile, blush, come alive, or nod in a shy manner, but they get it. It costs us nothing, takes so little time, and yet we get as much by giving this free gift to others as the recipient gets receiving. Try it.

EXERCISES

✳ ✳ ✳ ✳

Exercise 1—Learning to Give and Receive Feedback Powerfully

* The issue you need feedback on is: (e.g., I have a tense relationship with my daughter-in-law and I often end up in a disagreement).

* What type of feedback would be helpful for you right now (e.g., offer strategies to deal with difficult people)?

* Who in your circle of friends and colleagues could be helpful with that (e.g., my cousin in H.R., who is great at dealing with difficult people)?

* How will you ask her for feedback in a way that can help her help you (e.g., she's super busy, so I will ask her if she has fifteen minutes to offer suggestions on how to deal with difficult personalities)?

* How will you acknowledge her for being so helpful (e.g., she loves to laugh, so I'll make sure to send her funny videos and say "thanks for making me smile again—your advice was terrific!")?

REPEAT THE SAME PROCESS WHEN ASKED FOR FEEDBACK:

✳ Ask the person what type of feedback would be helpful. (Even if they don't know, it gives them a moment to start thinking about what they need, which is really helpful for both of you.)

✳ Be honest about whether you are the best person to give that feedback. If someone asks you for feedback on something you truly don't know about, you're not helping them or you.

✳ Give them the feedback they asked for in the most compassionate yet honest way you can, and be specific (e.g., telling someone to "not be so critical" of another person not as helpful as saying, "What upsets you most about this person?")

✳ Ask them if the feedback was helpful and in what way. You'll learn a lot about what they need and you'll strengthen your ability to give feedback.

Exercise 2—The Power of Acknowledgement

✳ Make it a habit to compliment or thank three people a day in a genuine, heartfelt way.

✳ Notice what happens with their voice or body language.

✳ Check in with yourself and see how it makes you feel.

✳ Do it every day for thirty days and see what happens.

✳ Be on the lookout for ways to compliment and acknowledge people. Nothing shifts your energy more!

Compliments and acknowledgments are totally free and invaluable. Both the giver and the receiver thrive in an environment of appreciation and acknowledgment.

Check-In

 * What really spoke to me about this Gem?

 * How can I apply it to my life?

 * What small action will I take NOW?

GEM 12

✳ ✳ ✳ ✳

THE 5CS OF CREATING A LIFE THAT LIGHTS YOU UP

Here we are and it's been a juicy ride! We've covered a lot of territory from Mining Your SPARKLE to Communication that Glistens and a whole lot more. I've run amok with my passions for acronyms, LOIS-isms, and a whole lot of content in service of supporting your most alive self. You've also rolled up your sleeves and done some deep work (either on paper or the reflective kind) on what living your most alive, authentic self looks and feels like for you, and what are the best actions to take in order to do that. It's been an honor and a privilege to have made this journey with you.

> ✳ **LOIS-ism**
>
> **Insights + Implementation = Incredible Results**

As promised, Courage to SPARKLE is a go-to Audacious Girl's guide to creating a Life that Lights You Up. While I am highly reflective and I see the enormous benefit that our insights can bring to our lives, unless we implement them they are just a lot of great "Aha" moments and won't bring much to the party. However, if we integrate our insights with implementation, incredible results are possible. Here's where my alliteration junkie will have one last spree: on how to use the 5Cs—Curiosity, Compassion, Connection, Course Correction, and Courage—to Create a Life that Lights You Up.

Curiosity

Curiosity saved my life and continues to save and enrich my life on a daily basis. I don't mean "saved my life" as if I'd be physically dead without it. But I certainly wouldn't be as alive and able to move forward with a specific type of engagement and pleasure without it. Curiosity has always led the way from my earliest exploration of what my Inner Critic looked like. It meshed with my day-to-day determination to look for luscious life lessons, even when they started out as lousy life lessons, and became a deep part of my growth both personally and professionally. Curiosity continues to play a huge role in my life. Curiosity leads the way in being fascinated by how we're wired as human beings as well as how to overcome one's obstacles and leverage one's gifts on a daily basis.

I believe we are all innately curious; it's simply been socialized out of some of us. Kids are naturally very curious. Children often say and do things that are "inconvenient" or "socially unacceptable" and when they do that, they nicely (if they're lucky) get their wrists slapped (metaphorically or otherwise). While it's important to have some decorum and play nice with the others in the sandbox of life, many of us get the message early on that curiosity will get us into trouble. Therefore, we shut down.

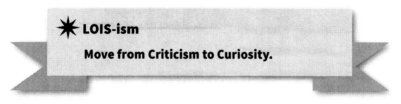

✳ LOIS-ism

Move from Criticism to Curiosity.

Curiosity affects my perspective the way that yoga affects one's body: it keeps us flexible, open, and allows us to move from a black-and-white view in life to all the colors of the rainbow. Curiosity makes my world a whole lot more interesting to live in. Curiosity is a daily practice, and it's the first step to creating a Life that Lights You Up. It does however take practice, and that's why I've provided an exercise at the end of this Gem to help you tap into your innate curiosity.

Next time you see yourself getting critical of yourself or others, take a moment to stop, breathe, and ask yourself: "How can I move from Criticism to Curiosity?"

REFLECTION QUESTIONS

1. Take something that is troubling you right now (aka Dimmers) and ask yourself: If I were to be curious about X, how might I approach it?

2. How might taking that approach make me feel?

3. What small action can I take?

Now look at a particular task or goal you have in your life (aka Shimmers) and ask yourself:

1. If I were to be curious about X, how might I approach this goal?

2. How might taking that approach make me feel?

3. What small action can I take?

Compassion

I'll repeat this over and over: criticism of ourselves and others constricts our spirits, our bodies, and our minds. Being compassionate toward others is not the same as condoning bad behavior, being a doormat, or going into denial. In addition, it's not about rationalizing our own behavior when we've made a mistake or acted inappropriately. Curiosity provides flexibility in the ways that we start to look at people and situations. Compassion provides a soft landing to open our hearts more, toward ourselves and others, while navigating life's sometimes seismic challenges.

Compassion toward Ourselves

We are often much more compassionate with others than we are with ourselves. I have one client who laughs sardonically and says, "If I treated others the way I treated myself, I'd have no friends." She's right and she's not alone. If you relate to my client and are really critical of yourself and have a hard time being compassionate, I'd start with treating and talking to yourself the way your BFF (or special person in your life who loves you dearly) does. At the end of this Gem, there is a meditation/ guided visualization that will help you cultivate compassion toward yourself.

As you are well aware of by now, I'm a huge fan of "part work" which is about isolating and identifying aspects of ourselves and seeing them as individual characters within us that need to be heard. Next time when you were angry at yourself or lack compassion take a couple of deep breaths. Imagine that scared little child within you who needs some love and guidance. I can almost guarantee that you'd start to soften how you talk to yourself. Start to befriend that part of you who is clearly crying out in pain or is frustrated or scared. Getting more critical will just make her feel worse.

Compassion toward Others

How easy it is to judge another's behavior when we don't know the full story of what they're going through. Where there's judgement, there's usually a short supply of compassion. Compassion is not about focusing on who's right and wrong, but actively stepping into someone else's experience and exhibiting an open heart.

I heard this great story that epitomizes compassion in action. It was a cold, rainy, dark night and two women got into a pretty bad fender bender. Thank goodness nobody got hurt and both cars were still in working condition. One woman came out of her car screaming at the other woman about what "she had done." The other woman stood quietly, listened, and didn't defend or agree. Once the woman who was screaming stopped, the other woman looked her in the eye and in the most compassionate way said, "Look, we're two women alone on a desolate road in the middle of the night who had an unfortunate accident. We're very lucky that neither one of us got hurt and that our cars are still working. Let's work together, so we can remedy the situation and get home safe." The other woman's anger melted and she agreed. They handled the rest of the incident as peacefully as they could and went on their ways.

One could say that the second woman had great communication skills or had the soundness of mind to address the unfortunate incident with a level head, and you'd be right. What spoke to me the most was when she said, "we're two women." Giving voice to both their humanity and vulnerability in that moment, allowed the other woman to shift. She leveled the playing field, softened her heart, and they both recognized that they were struggling with the same thing.

That's where the real power of compassion manifests itself. Compassion wakes our heart up to the fact that most of the time we're doing the best we can, with what we've got, given wherever we are in our lives. Compassion gives us front row seats to both our own and others' humanity and often our fragility. The more we look at what the other person may be going through, the easier we can view them through the lens of compassion and the more we can be in their world.

REFLECTION QUESTIONS

1. Take something that is troubling you right now (aka Dimmers) and ask yourself: If I were to be compassionate toward X, how might I approach this issue differently?

2. How might taking that approach make me feel?

3. What small action can I take?

Now look at something you're really excited about accomplishing in your life and ask yourself:

1. What would be the most compassionate approach I can take toward reaching my goal?

2. How might taking that approach make me feel?

3. What small action can I take?

Connection

We've spoken about many different ways to stay connected with the multiple aspects of yourself: first, how to identify your SPARKLE (Gem 1—Mining for Your SPARKLE) second, honoring your wiring (Gem 6—Illuminating Your Unique Wiring) third, keeping your energy focused (Gem 9—From Dimmers to Shimmers) and finally, building your Team SPARKLE (Gem 10—Creating a Scintillating Circle of Support). These are all different ways to connect with yourself and others. Here are some ways to do just that.

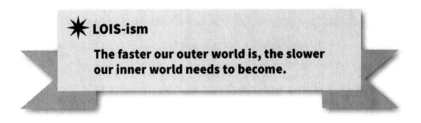

✴ LOIS-ism

The faster our outer world is, the slower our inner world needs to become.

Connect with Ourselves

STOP. Close your eyes. Breathe. Feel. Repeat. Do this as often as possible. The more frantic our outside world becomes, the more we need to stop and breathe to return to our center. Give yourself a break and regroup. There are a boatload of different ways to take care of yourself that we've spoken about. Nothing can substitute for making a choice to be present. If you go through these four steps consciously three to five times a day for one minute each, you'll be amazed how different you'll start to feel. One of the most important ways to connect is to be very clear about where you want your focus to be and then put your attention there. It's not an exact science, and it won't happen overnight. The clearer you are about who you are, and the more you honor it, the deeper the connection you'll have with your spirit, your passion, and your SPARKLE.

Connect with our Truth

I do believe that our body is hardwired with a BS meter that tells us when something feels right and when it feels wrong. Take a moment when your body gives you a signal, whether it's a "yum" or "yuck," and listen to it. While I'm a very reflective person by nature, and can be quite analytical, it has always been the signals in my body that have been my own GPS. They let me know when I am on and off track, as well as which people have tribe potential and which aren't. Listen. The more we learn to really trust ourselves and listen to that "little voice of instinct," the louder and more pronounced that voice becomes.

Connect with Others

There are many different ways to connect with others that can build important relationships. We've addressed this a lot in Gem 10—Creating a Scintillating Circle of Support and Gem 11—Communication that Glistens, in addition to providing many tools that are sprinkled throughout the book. We need different types of connections at different times in our life, both personally and professionally. Build your community and reach out to them in a way that is helpful, fulfilling, and be available for them to reach out to you.

Find Little Ways of Making Meaningful Connections

Find a way to connect that is truly fulfilling and fun for you. It may be sending a card, giving a quick compliment, or picking up the phone and saying, "I had ten minutes and wanted to say hi." It doesn't matter; it's the quality not the quantity.

While writing this book, I learned the impact of making brief but quite lovely connections. As I got close to my lifeline (LOIS-ism for deadline) for this book, I would spend entire days in front of the computer and didn't see a soul all day. Many an email text or phone call may have been exchanged, but I had very little in-person contact. I was not lonely because I was in the world of my book, but I was clearly alone. During the last several weeks, I frequented a relatively healthy fast food place right next door, where I'd get my roasted chicken and veggies on a fairly consistent basis.

Being my mother's daughter, I would strike up conversations with many of the very friendly servers. There was one in particular, though, who really made me feel special. A young man named Wade would see me coming and by the time I got to the counter, he had not only put in my order that he had memorized, but my "tasting menu" (a small sample cup of saffron rice, mashed potatoes, and corn) was almost always waiting for me. I'd joke with him by calling it that; the irony of a "tasting menu" for a fast food joint was not wasted on either one of us. Hector, the man behind the grill would call out 'Hello, half-chicken-all-dark-all-thighs lady!,' which made me smile while other customers would just scratch their heads in confusion. I would take my cornbread to go in a separate bag and scout out the "dining in" patrons. I'd casually go up to a table and say, "Hi, would you like to have my extra cornbread?" For the most part (I did have a few occasional odd looks) they would light up and graciously accepted it. Yes, we all love free food, but it was that someone thought of them and extended themselves. The whole encounter took about ten minutes at the most.

I felt energized, and it was my version of my afternoon coffee break. It helped to launch part two of my writing day. I was reminded of the power of connection, even on a very small level, and the rich experience of what both giving and receiving can provide to making our days a tad more magical.

REFLECTION QUESTIONS (DIMMERS)

1. When I do _____, I feel connected with my SPARKLE.

2. One way I can connect with others when I'm feeling alone and isolated is_____.

3. I always know something rings true for me when I _____
   _____.

REFLECTION QUESTIONS (SHIMMERS)

1. When I do _____, I feel more connected with my SPARKLE.

2. One way I enjoy connecting with others is _____.

3. I always know something rings true for me when I _____
   _____.

Course Correction

There are times we feel off-course in our lives. It's just part of life. If we stay off-course for too long, however, we'll end up on Dimmers—end of story. Here are some principles and tools that will help you Course Correct when you're feeling disconnected from your SPARKLE. Pick which ones resonate for you and experiment with them.

Sailing is Off-Course Most of the Time

When you are sailing, you are never going in a straight line. The earth is not flat and the wind does not blow in only one direction. In sailing against the wind (or the obstacles of our life), we often have to tack in a zig-zag course that feels like two steps forward, one step back. If you are going to reach your destination, most likely it will be a non-linear trajectory to get wherever "there" is. Very little of life truly is linear and yet we consistently want our progress to be linear. Sailing depends largely on one's relationship to the wind, where we need to course correct in order to work in partnership with it. The same is true for our life journey. There will always be factors out of our control. When we embrace those parts of life that we have no control over and make choices that serve our most authentic selves, we end up in a far better place. How can you embrace the non-linear aspect of your life right now and Course Correct in order to use it to your benefit?

Feedback versus Failure

Every time we take an action, whatever the action is, there's an outcome or result connected to that action. We have a choice at any moment to interpret that result in a certain way. While we're disappointed when we take an action and it doesn't go our way, it's too easy to consider a string of disappointments as a failure. I would highly encourage you to look at the results in your life as a series of feedback opportunities. When we look at life's experiences that way, we are able to refine, adjust accordingly, and create a life that lights us up.

I had the honor of meeting and sitting down with Dr. Joel N. Myers, a meteorologist who is the founder, president, and chairman of the board of AccuWeather, Inc., an American commercial weather service. AccuWeather provides forecasts and data to over 175,000 clients around the world and serves millions. Dr. Myers is considered one of the top 500 entrepreneurs in the world. He knew he wanted to be a meteorologist from the age of seven. He was such a smart kid, a plethora of well-meaning yet protective people in his life encouraged him instead to go into other professions that had more potential financial success. From his nickname, "One-Track-Mind Joel," it was clear that nothing was going to stop him. In talking with him, it was clear that he was tenacious and passionate about bringing the most accurate weather predictions and resources to companies and industries where having accurate weather was foundational to the success of their businesses (e.g., ski resorts, farming, manufacturing). He was equally passionate about bringing that information to individuals as well.

What stood out the most was his absolute clarity from the get-go about the level of resistance he knew that he was going to be up against. From day one, he was well aware that he would be charging fees for something that companies and entire industries had received for free, for decades. Armed with lists of thousands of potential customers, he pursued them one at a time. On occasion, he did feel discouraged by the thousands of rejections, but he leveraged his tenacity and confidence to get through. He kept using the feedback he received to gain more accuracy with his weather projections and course correct his approach accordingly. He became not only very successful but also created the impact and value for his customers that he was passionate about providing.

This story reinforces the truth that when we make a choice to stand out, to share our gifts, to celebrate who we are however big or small, there will often be pushback. There almost has to be when we're pushing against the old paradigm of how things were in place of how things can possibly be. Every pioneer or innovator is told in one way or another "You can't do it." But what is really often true is, "it's just never been done."

Maybe you're a rabble-rouser or just want to make some subtle but powerful shifts in your life or in your community. Either way, you can rest assured that if you're not simply phoning in your life, you will get pushback. There will be resistance, most likely internally and externally. In that moment, you have an extraordinary opportunity to interpret that response as "failure," "resistance," or "pushback"—or as "feedback" that you can interpret and use to course correct. However, when we look through the lens of feedback versus failure and course correct accordingly, we are most likely in a better place to make choices that lead to living a life that holds meaning for us.

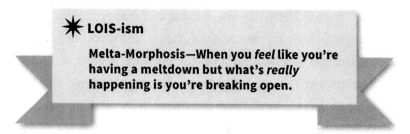

LOIS-ism

Melta-Morphosis—When you *feel* like you're having a meltdown but what's *really* happening is you're breaking open.

I'm not Falling Apart, I'm Breaking Open

I had to remind myself that on a regular basis between January 1st, 2015 to mid-2016. We are going through seismic changes on both a planetary as well as personal level, and I am no different.

After spearheading the hospice care for my mom, Edie, for two years alongside my brother and sister, I left a loving, but not right, twelve-and-a-half-year relationship with my partner, Charlie. I lost the office that we shared. I became estranged from a previously close family member and my business, which had been running quite smoothly for years, seemed to cycle off. My life, in short, caved in on itself and became unrecognizable to me. Sometimes, I wanted to give both myself and my life a nametag so I could readily identify who both of us were. There were days where I woke up and, joking around with the PTB (powers that be), I'd say, "Well, I don't have bed bugs, Lyme disease, or identity theft, so the day is off to a good start." I was reminded by friends to "never ask the universe, 'what else *now*?' because you may not like the response you get."

I'm not sharing any of this to gain any airtime on the sympathy channel from you, I assure you. I am aware of all the ways I'm exceedingly lucky and deeply blessed. I have my health—something I never take for granted. I have dear friends and a wonderful family. I have a very comfortable home. I have work that I truly love. I am also hardwired to seek out the life lesson even when things start out really lousy (which, believe me, they often did). Sometimes this assessment was a day at a time, other times, a moment at a time.

When I share my journey with the groups I speak to, I witness a sea of nodding heads. People share with me their own, often haunting, stories of the ways their lives have caved in on them and often scary periods of uncertainty, they're going through. Many of us are going through major changes in our lives, which sometimes means we feel more off-course than ever. I get it.

As I am finishing the last Gem in this book, while there have been exceedingly difficult times over the last eighteen months, it's been one of the most important times in my life. It's been a time of countless miracles, gifts, learning, and new opportunities that I would never have dreamed were possible. However, none of these would've shown up if I hadn't allowed myself to go through the process I went through and give myself some time to fall apart...before I could break open. There is so much that I learned and continue to learn that I could share. So if you are feeling like you're falling apart but actually are breaking open, I offer these principles and suggestions that made a huge difference for me and I hope will for you on the subject of Course Correction.

Let life get messy. No matter how much you plan and take action, both of which are important, you must allow your life (feelings, circumstances, and relationships) to get "messy." By messy, I mean that you'll probably feel disoriented, confused, and in unfamiliar territory since you've never undertaken this chapter of your life before. If you insist that your life has to look a certain way, you'll continue to feel frustrated and off-track like you're doing it wrong. It'll only exacerbates your anxiety. In my own life, I kept thinking of all the things I should be doing, the actions I needed to take to get back on track with my business and other areas of my life, but ultimately it was a way of trying to go back to what would never be. While I'm a huge proponent of taking action, when you're doing it to just maintain the illusion of control, it won't take you far.

When I finally surrendered to the fact that I didn't have a template for SPARKLE 2.0, let things get messy, allowed myself to not have all the answers, and not be such a smarty pants all the time, that's when my life started opening up. When I discovered that I couldn't do all the things I did before in order to reboot this new chapter of my life, I had to let myself not know for a while.

In Grief, there's Relief. I saw this postcard in a trendy San Francisco card shop twenty years ago and it's stayed with me ever since. No matter what the circumstances are that are contributing to you no longer recognizing your life, it's imperative to grieve. We live in a culture that provides limited space or tolerance for grieving. We're too quick to slap on a happy Band-Aid of "look on the bright side" or "this too shall pass." *These are sound principles, once* you've been through the heavy lifting of grieving, but there's no short cut. Grieving is not the same as bellyaching, being a victim, falling into a bottomless pit of self-pity or TMI-ing on different social media channels. Those all just keep the drama going. It's being willing to face the feelings of a chapter of your life closing that has a significant amount of loss attached to it.

LOIS-ism

They Don't Call it a Good Cry for Nothing.

I'm still amazed by how embarrassed we all are when we cry. I LOVE crying. It's my way of giving my eyeballs a bath and my soul a reprieve. Emotional tears from both strife and laughter actually help clear stress toxins from your body. Tears on all levels are one of the great gifts of being alive. While you may opt not to cry in certain environments, make sure to give yourself a nurturing environment in which to let out the tears.

Create a safe and loving community. I addressed this in Gem 10—Creating Your Scintillating Circle of Support. Even if you're an introvert and/or a private person, it's essential to not go through either the joys or sorrows of your life alone. There's nothing especially noble about being in isolation and doing it on your own. We're the most social creatures on the planet. We need each other. Going through the breaking-open process in a community allows us the gift of being witnessed. Your community doesn't have to have a lot of people. It just needs to be *your* tribe, people with whom you feel safe, seen, and loved. Go to people who can give you what you need and be there for others.

Look for the Lesson. Amidst the messiness of life when we're going through major changes, there are always lessons to be learned. Keep on the lookout. One of my daily, simple prayers is: "What do I need to learn from this experience?" There's always a lesson. It will seldom come when we ask for it, but it shows up when we least expect it—like love. Looking for the lessons is not about taking a shortcut around our process, but rather giving us a context for learning. We can "grow" through the change versus "go" through the change. No matter what is going on in your life, ask yourself, "What can I learn through this experience?"

Humor is the salve that heals all wounds. There are always opportunities to laugh and learn even when you're in pain. Look for them. Life is one of the most absurd and ironic adventures. Look for the laughter and you'll find it. It lightens the load.

On the way back from my Grandma Lily's (my maternal grandmother) funeral, my mother, who had a devastatingly painful relationship with her mother, started laughing hysterically. Mom, who had the sharpest sense of humor of anyone I know, turned to me and said, "Two more things that Grandma is now *really* pissed off at me for. No A/C in the hearse and the food at the *shiva* was lousy. She really *is* rolling in her grave." My entire family laughed so hard that tears started streaming down our faces. The hearse driver turned around and said, "It's always healing to recollect fond memories of our loved ones," which of course, made us laugh even harder. No matter what you're going through, never lose your sense of humor, you can find it in the irony and absurdity of life.

You're your own role model. As I mentioned in Gem 6—Illuminating Your Unique Wiring, while it's great to look to others as role models, you ultimately are your own role model. You are far more resilient and resourceful than you give yourself credit for. You may not have ever gone through the changes you're going through, but you have life experience to draw upon that got you through. Take out that Evidence List. Remind yourself not only that you don't have to do it alone but you have a storehouse of life experiences and resources within you that will get you to the next chapter. Ask people who really know you to remind you of what kind of a rock star you are and of your Courage to SPARKLE.

Embrace the blank slate. There's something both daunting and dazzling about a blank slate. You get to create whatever you want. When you approach your blank slate from a place of curiosity and intrigue about what makes you SPARKLE, then it's an exciting and exhilarating process. When you approach it with dread and feelings of being overwhelmed, life puts you on Dimmers. "What's Next?" can be asked from a state of upset or excitement—you get to choose. Allowing yourself to "not know" for awhile can be a very powerful way to usher in a new chapter of our life. Most of us experience "I don't know," with anxiety and that's pretty common. But sometimes, not knowing can provide enormous freedom. What would your life look like if you embraced a blank slate?

Be open to new possibilities. During my eighteen-plus months of not recognizing my life, several opportunities opened up for me that I've been wanting to explore for several years but passed on because it just wasn't the right time. One was launching my own You Tube video series, which was a combination of Wayne Dyer (grandfather of personal growth) and Carol Burnett (grandma of a comedy variety and heartfelt sketch comedy). I tried to launch it four years ago, but it never felt right. During this crazy time of my upside-down, hardly recognizable life, my videographer/editor, director, two assistants who would become my script supervisor, prop maker, and costume/prop person, all fell together effortlessly and helped me create *SMART SEXY*

TV: What Nobody Talks About...But Everyone Needs to Hear. Three months later, my publisher approached me to write this book. It's something I've been wanting to do for a while. Shortly after that, a collaborative partnership emerged with my long-standing friend and colleague, Elizabeth Browning, to collectively support women and our *Shatter Your Inner Glass Ceiling Programs* came to be.

When we're in the same ol' same ol' and life is just moving along, we are not as loose and flexible to take advantage of opportunities as when we are both falling apart and breaking open, that's where the magic happens.

REFLECTION

1. What small action can you take to Course Correct right now?
2. When will you take it?
3. How can you celebrate your resiliency and resourcefulness?

Courage

Ah, our last tasty C of the 5Cs! Courage, big or small, occupies a special sunroom in my heart. Courage comes from the Latin word for heart, "cor." In one of its earliest forms, the word courage meant "to speak one's mind by telling all one's heart." I love that definition. I'd broaden its interpretation to mean telling all one's heart, not only with our words and actions, but with our passions, our hungers, and our light.

I have the supreme honor of having a front row seat to seeing my client's dreams manifest. It's the best seat in town. Some of them are big epic dreams, others are small but just as mighty, many are affairs of the heart, and still others are about birthing their most authentic selves. They all matter. This is one of my favorite experiences as a coach. This is a story of Courage.

Andrea, a twenty-three-year-old, walked into my office with her big saucer eyes that looked very sad. She felt she had unwittingly given up her dream of being a veterinarian by letting her grades slip through her four years during her Ivy League college education. A combination of being away from home the first time, not understanding the rigor it took to excel as a pre-med, and perhaps getting too involved in her social life as a sorority sister, were to blame. A classic case of "didn't know what you didn't know," which unfortunately in life, is often the scenario that gets us the most; especially, when we discover it too late.

By the time she came to me, Andrea had traded in her "I can be anything" hopes of her dream profession and for an "alternative" (code word for less desirable) career in medicine. While other classmates were either going off to medical school, getting graduate degrees, or jetting into their careers, she took on the heroic act of giving herself a do-over. She enrolled in a two-year, post-baccalaureate program, hoping that the increase in her GPA in her major (science) would be a game changer. She was even willing to rack up additional school loans in the process.

We worked together for about nine months. Andrea got her studying and rigor back on track and she made sure to have a few internships with local animal shelters as well as in veterinarian's offices. She did this while holding down a full-time job in hospitality, and advocating for and transporting her mom to oncologists after she was diagnosed with cancer. Clearly, she was a rock star.

As the universe is known to do, it "conspires to support us" when we make a commitment from our heart and take the actions to back it up! Through a sorority sister, Andrea found out that there was a university with a vet program that was forgiving of smart students who didn't have top grades but are very committed to changing that. The day had come where all her hard work, dreams, and sweat equity paid off. They offered her an interview. It was a longshot but still in the realm of possibility for her to be accepted.

Andrea worked tirelessly on her interview skills, preparing her mock interview. I asked her all the really hard questions and we brainstormed the best way to answer them. Roleplay and mock interviews are some of the most important tools when looking to advance one's self. All of your negative self-talk comes up and you get to make the worst mistakes on the dress rehearsal. The great news is that the nervous system doesn't know the difference between a dream rehearsal and opening night. By practicing ahead of time, your nervousness naturally dissipates.

I asked her the hardest question right out of the gate while role-playing as the interviewer: "Andrea, I see while you were an undergraduate you had a C+ average. Why was it so low? Even though you got it up to a 3.2 with your post-baccalaureate program, how can we be assured you will maintain those grades, and even improve them, if we accept you into our veterinarian program?"

She started off as expected, talking about it being the first time away from home, the adjustment being difficult, and not having developed the study skills that she needed. It wasn't bad but it didn't bring in her humanity, her overall feistiness, and the full circle approach she had taken in her process. I urged Andrea to talk more about the lessons she learned. She got quiet. She felt embarrassed by the choices she had made and was reluctant to share them.

Sure enough, when she did the actual interview, the interviewer asked her the infamous question about her prior grades. This time, Andrea looked up at him and thanked him for bringing it up because she was planning to volunteer that information had he not. She shared the life lessons that she learned over the last six years from letting her grades fall way behind to rebooting her commitment to doing whatever it took to go for her dreams. She shared the price of "not knowing what she didn't know" and the importance of taking responsibility but never giving up. Andrea went to great lengths to talk about how she had to learn how to study, her commitment to it, and that ultimately, she gave herself a second chance and hoped that he would, too. She plugged in some good Brag Bites (what Peggy Klaus refers to in her book, "BRAG!) on how she had close to a 4.0 in her post-baccalaureate program while holding down multiple internships, working a full-time job in hospitality, and still advocating for her mom's care.

She ended by saying that even though it took tremendous time, energy, and focus to turn things around, had she not fallen behind she never would have learned both how precious one's dreams are and the importance of committing to them 1000%. While she didn't regret what had happened, she knew what to do in order for it to never happen again. With great clarity and dignity, she promised him that if they accepted her into the program, she'd give it her full commitment. Andrea also emphasized her commitment to helping those around her to not make the same mistakes she had made in her earlier years. In her final comments, she reiterated that she had given herself "a second chance" and she hoped they would, too.

When Andrea finished her response the interviewer, had tears in his eyes. He looked away because he didn't want her to see how emotional he had gotten by her heartfelt answer. He finally turned to her, smiled, and said "I can get in trouble for this. This has been one of the best interviews I've ever had with an applicant. I'm going to recommend that you be accepted into the program. I think you'll be an enormous asset to the college. However, I can't guarantee that you'll be admitted." She smiled thanked him profusely and shook his hand very hard.

That was several years ago. Andrea did get into that school, and a few years ago, we met for lunch. At the time, she was a junior at the university, had a 4.0 GPA, was a T.A. for two courses, and still found time to tutor a few students. She still had those big saucer eyes but they were no longer sad. She loved her school, the program, and most of all, couldn't wait to be a vet. Andrea is now a full-fledged veterinarian who graduated with honors and is interning at several hospitals and is passionate about her work.

Courage is equal parts determination, passion, and vulnerability. Miracles happen when you are courageous. Be authentic. Let people fall in love with you.

Think of how amazing our lives, our communities, and the world would start to look like if we, collectively, allowed others to fall in love with us, by sharing our dreams, and supported each other in the Courage to SPARKLE!

EXERCISES

✳   ✳   ✳   ✳

Exercise 1—The 5Cs

PART 1—WHEN ON DIMMERS

Stop. Close Your Eyes. Breathe. Feel. Stay in your body.

1. **Curiosity**—What's going on right now for me (e.g., feelings, experiences, insights)? What can I learn from this challenge right now?

2. **Compassion**—If my BFF (or someone who consistently has your back) was speaking to me, what would be the kindest, most loving thing they would say? How would they tell me to take care of myself? How can I integrate their voice into my own life?

3. **Connection**—What is the most productive way to stay connected with myself? My truth? Others in my life?

4. **Course Correction**—How might I feel off-track? What action can I take to course correct (remember: acceptance is an action)?

5. **Courage**—What am I most afraid of? What is an action I can take in the face of my fear that serves me?

PART 2—WHEN ON SHIMMERS

Stop. Close Your Eyes. Breathe. Feel. Stay in your body.

1. **Curiosity**—What's going on right now for me (e.g., feelings, experiences, insights)? What can I learn from this blessing right now?

2. **Compassion**—If my BFF (or someone who consistently has your back) was speaking to me, how would they help me celebrate this gift in my life? In what loving ways would they support me to take care of myself? How can I give that to myself?

3. **Connection**—How can I stay connected with myself to really take in this blessing? What rings true to me? How can I celebrate with others?

4. **Course Correction**—How might I still feel off-track? What action can I take to course correct (sometimes letting yourself receive is an action)?

5. **Courage**—How have I been courageous? What will be my next courageous action?

Exercise 2—Cultivating Curiosity

1. Take one thing in your life that you're really curious about. You may have a lot of experience in this area (e.g., like fixing things, the origins of words, history); it doesn't matter what.

2. Set a timer for five minutes and immerse yourself in that activity.

3. Go back and set aside another five minutes and do it again, but now watch yourself being curious. What does it look like? What are the thoughts you have? What's your process in pursuing your curiosity? In my case, I'm a connector, I'm always connecting ideas, concepts, sequences, patterns, and people. I have a pattern-seeking chip in my brain that will always look for connections. So when I am curious, I'm always looking for the connections.

4. Find a neutral item, set a timer for another five minutes and "get curious." Neutral items like a paper clip, statue, or even a greeting card, are great primers for developing curiosity because they are not emotionally charged at all. It's a lot easier to nurture curiosity when you're not biased or have a strong emotional charge. Let's say you pick a paper clip, which seems ridiculously mundane, and ask yourself, "Hmmm how was it made? How many people were responsible for making it? How many documents and what kind of documents will it hold in its 'life time'"?

Now, many of you you may be thinking, "What? I've got to look at a paper clip and get curious about it in order to create a Life that Lights Me Up?" Yes. I find that the more we can cultivate curiosity in the most mundane ways and about the most mundane things, the more resources we have when the heavy lifting of life comes our way in the form of Dimmers. The more we can start to look at what we can learn in any and all situations in our lives, the more we can make a bold and audacious step in productive thinking and action.

Exercise 3—Developing Compassion toward Yourself

1. What are a few challenges in your life that could use a healthy dose of compassion right now (e.g., being more compassionate about how much I'm juggling and patient with getting things done)?

2. What is the meanest thing you say to yourself on a daily basis (e.g., I'm just a mess and can never seem to get it together, I'll never achieve what I want)?

3. If you brought in your Inner BFF, how would change that conversation (e.g., I notice that I am often putting other people's commitments before my own)?

4. Take an action on behalf of yourself. Any action that speaks to you.

Exercise 4—Compassion Meditation

I see most of us "adults" as little children dressed up in "grown up" bodies. Visualizing us all this way connects me with compassion very easily. While we may take on very senior leadership positions and have inordinate responsibilities, the part of us that gets our feelings hurt and is most damaged by self-criticism is the little kid part of us. Take a moment and do a Compassion Check-in first toward yourself and then toward others. Connect with that compassionate self and send loving vibes to a part of you that may be struggling, or to someone around you who is in pain. See what starts to shift in your life.

Check-In

* What resonated for you about the 5Cs?
* How will you use it?
* What one small step can you take to experience the Courage to SPARKLE?

AFTERWORD

✳ ✳ ✳ ✳

COURAGE TO SPARKLE—IT'S A MOVEMENT.

While on paper we appear to be nearing the end of *Courage to SPARKLE: The Audacious Girls' Guide to Creating a Life that Lights You Up*, I see it as more of a beginning. The beginning of an important conversation of support for each other, as women, to shine brightly in the world with our gifts and our passions, and the beginning of actively pursuing a life of meaning and fulfillment. Not only will we be the beneficiaries, the world around us also gets elevated through our own SPARKLE.

There are so many ways to continue this vital conversation and engagement in the world, many of which you're probably already doing. It's all very important work. I want to point out one of the most foundational pieces of the Courage to SPARKLE movement, which, is illustrated with a story.

A little less than a year ago, I was getting my annual mammogram at my local imaging center. I was in the waiting room with about six other women, all in our medical "gowns" waiting to be called in. It started with a woman who was reading a magazine article about this controversial book from a female author, who urged women to push past their barriers in the workplace so they could elevate themselves professionally. The woman started trashing the author, saying totally inaccurate things about her background as well as the practical applications of her expertise. Clearly wanting to rally the others in the waiting room, she looked around for their nodding heads of approval.

At first, I was enraged. I knew that what she was saying was totally wrong since I had recently finished the book and had taken copious notes on it. In my mind, the author was extremely brave and generous. This was a woman who could've easily thought, "Hey, I'm sitting pretty; why upset the apple cart and become a potential target for haters?" But she didn't. Instead, she spoke her truth, but more importantly, gave great advice to women about taking the next step in advocating for themselves. She accumulated a lot of fans, but almost as many naysayers and haters. I still applaud her for her courage.

I didn't want to get into an argument with the woman in the waiting room, especially given how vulnerable we all were dressed in our medical garb, but I felt like I had to say something. I breathed several times to calm myself down and simply asked her, "Did you actually *read* the book?" She dodged the question, avoided my eyes, talked to the *others* about all the reviews and excerpts that she read—which of course, out of context, are often very skewed— insisting that she "knew" about the book.

In a very diplomatic way, I kept asking the same question. "But did you actually *read* the entire book?" She finally admitted she hadn't. I looked her in the eyes and with as much compassion as I could muster certainly not wanting to shame her, and I said, "Please don't do that. Please don't talk against women who are trying to elevate other women. Please don't spread uninformed opinions that shoot down other women's efforts to excel. It's okay if you disagree. You're allowed to have a different point of view. But be informed if you're going to speak against another sister who's trying desperately to help women shatter the Glass Ceiling. We need each other more than ever." She got quiet. She looked away and nodded "yes," and the others went back to their respective magazines. But I knew from the looks on their faces they got the message, too.

I didn't speak out to that woman to ridicule or embarrass her, but to make a point: to send a message that "we need each other." We need each other to support each other, more than ever. If we are going to Shatter the Outer Glass Ceiling amongst us all, we need to Shatter the Inner Glass Ceiling within us all along with it. We need our sisters and brothers to help us on that journey. We need to celebrate all those who make an honest effort to accomplish that.

Idle damaging gossip that puts down the truly earnest efforts of someone else is a lot like crack. It's a cheap and easy high. When we are feeling not great about ourselves or threatened by possible changes in the world, it's too easy to shoot others down. It's being spiritually lazy. You're off the hook. All you have to do is open your mouth and talk smack. It's really addictive and seductive, but it's ultimately expensive to all of us.

It sends a negative message to women of all generations: If you stand out in a way that elevates you, as a woman, you'll be shot down. You'll be given a lot of nasty adjectives next to your name. Much of the name-calling will be from other women. From there, we will start down the same ol' same ol' road to resignation: "Why bother? It will never happen anyway." Lastly, it sends a message to men that women cannot support each other and gives them permission to tear us down, too. So toxic! I'm a huge proponent of activism on so many levels, and sometimes the greatest act of activism we can participate in is monitoring what comes out of our own mouth on a moment-to-moment basis. Let's support each other in this mission to shine in the world and celebrate the many men amongst us (and there are many) and women, who also want to support women, both personally and professionally.

I am a softie at heart. Through the years, I've fallen in love with songs or quotes that start a trend of kindness and benevolence in the world. Even if it's short-lived, it's still a step. From the movement that started with that simple jewel of a quote, "Practice random kindness and senseless acts of beauty" to the happy song of almost every decade from, "We are the World" to "Don't Worry Be Happy" to the most recent hit tune "Happy," there is a reason they all go viral. We are more ravenous than ever for a sense of kindness and optimism in the world.

A friend of mine ran into Gloria Steinem at an event, when her daughter was about sixteen years old. She introduced her daughter to Ms. Steinem and said, "Honey, do you know who Gloria Steinem is?" Her daughter felt a tad embarrassed and shrugged her shoulders, "No." Steinem smiled, looked her straight in the eye and said, "It's not important that you know who *I* am. But it's *very* important you know who *you* are." What a powerful example of taking one moment out and elevating another woman in such a simple, elegant way.

If all we did was to take a moment to support ourselves and each other in our Courage to SPARKLE in the world, in small or big ways, we'd see a huge paradigm shift within a very short period of time.

Let's do it!

SPARKLE ON!

Lois

ABOUT THE AUTHOR

✳ ✳ ✳ ✳

Lois Barth, Human Development Expert, Motivational Speaker, Whole Life Coach, and author of *Courage to SPARKLE: The Audacious Girls' Guide to Creating a Life that Lights You Up*, brings more than twenty-five years of combined experience as a speaker, coach, actress, comedienne, singer, arts educator and health care practitioner to the party.

Often referred to as the "Bette Midler of Women's Empowerment," Lois uses humor, stories, and science in her high-energy interactive programs to help her audiences fire their inner perfectionist, turn lousy life lessons into luscious life lessons, and get out of their "familiarity zones" so they can have the Courage to SPARKLE. She not only shares her professional expertise but uses the same principles and techniques that have been instrumental in helping her to maintain a thirty-five-pound weight loss for over twenty years, overcome debilitating stage fright and chronic negative self-talk, and navigate the rocky road of career challenges and running her own business.

Lois has a B.S. in Human Development, multiple coaching certifications, is a licensed massage therapist, and was the life coach for three national makeover campaigns: *SELF, Fitness*, and FITSTUDIO (Sears) in which, thus far, 1.8 million people have participated in. She is the creator of *SMART SEXY TV: What Nobody Talks About But Needs To Hear*, her own YouTube series which brings a humorous, light-hearted approach to communication, motivation, and empowerment. Lois was the

"Stress Less...SPARKLE More" Lady for C.T. Style TV (ABC affiliate) and has been published and quoted in the *New York Times, Wall Street Journal, Woman's Day*, and Elle.com, to name a few. She has spoken to groups at L'Oréal, the Red Cross, Capital One Bank, the Society of Women Engineers, and the United States Navy, amongst many others. She is a contributing writer for three anthologies: *Have I Got a Guy For You, Empowering Women,* and *Money Talks; 100 Strategies to Master Tricky Conversations about Money.*

To learn more about her Courage to SPARKLE keynote, workshops trainings, and coaching, please go to www.loisbarth.com.

COURAGE TO SPARKLE RESOURCES

✳ ✳ ✳ ✳

These books, CDs, DVDs, and websites are suggested to augment and deepen the information and principles discussed in each GEM.

Gem 1—Mining for Your SPARKLE

Beck, Martha. *Finding Your Own North Star: Claiming the Life You Were Meant to Live.* New York: Crown Publishing Group, 2002.

Fortgang, Laura Berman. *Now What? Revised Edition: 90 Days to a New Life Direction.* New York: Jeremy P. Tarcher/Penguin, 2015.

LaPorte, Danielle. *The Desire Map: A Guide to Creating Goals with Soul.* Boulder, CO: Sounds True, 2014.

Sinetar, Marsha. *Do What You Love, the Money Will Follow: Discovering Your Right Livelihood.* New York: Dell, 1989.

Gem 2—Don't Backburner the Bright Light That is You!

Roth, Geneen. *Feeding the Hungry Heart: The Experience of Compulsive Eating.* New York: Plume, 1993.

Rubin, Gretchen. *The Happiness Project (Revised Edition): Or, Why I spent a Year Trying to Sing in the Morning, Clean My Closets, Fight Right, Read Aristotle, and Generally Have More Fun.* New York: HarperCollins, 2015.

Williamson, Marianne. *A Return to Love: Reflections on the Principles of "A Course in Miracles."* New York: HarperCollins, 1996.

Gem 3—Let Your Audacious Self Shine Through

Beck, Martha. *Steering by Starlight: The Science and Magic of Finding Your Destiny.* New York: Rodale Books, 2009.

Robbins, Mike. *Be Yourself, Everyone Else is Already Taken: Transform Your Life with the Power of Authenticity.* San Francisco: Jossey-Bass, 2009.

SARK. *Living Juicy: Daily Morsels for Your Creative Soul.* Berkeley, CA: Celestial Arts, 1994.

———. *Succulent Wild Women: Dancing with Your Wonder-Full Self!* New York: Simon & Schuster, 1997.

Stanfield, Jana. *Brave Faith.* Jana Stan Tunes, 1998. *CD* and *MP3.*

West, Mae, and Susanna Clapp. *Goodness Had Nothing to Do With It.* Englewood Cliffs, NJ: Prentice-Hall, 1959. OUT OF PRINT.

Gem 4—Bring Your Darkness into the Light

Browning, Elizabeth. *Transformational Acting Exercises for Life.* DVD. http://www.elizabethbrowning.com/

Ford, Debbie. *The Dark Side of the Light Chasers: Reclaiming Your Power, Creativity, Brilliance and Dreams.* New York: Riverhead Books, 2010.

Miller, Alice. *The Drama of the Gifted Child: The Search for the True Self.* Revised and Updated Edition. New York: Basic Books, 1997.

St. James, Aleta. *Life Shift: Let Go and Live Your Dream.* New York: Fireside, 2005.

Gem 5—Lighten Up While You Learn

Carter, Judy. *The Message of You: Turn Your Life Story Into a Money-Making Speaking Career.* New York: St. Martin's Press, 2013.

God Said Ha! Dir. Julia Sweeney. Perf. Julia Sweeney, Quentin Tarantino. Miramax, 2003. DVD.

Johnson, Spencer. *Who Moved My Cheese? An Amazing Way to Deal with Change in Your Work and in Your Life.* New York: G.P. Putnam's Sons, 1998.

Lamott, Anne. *Operating Instructions: A Journal of My Son's First Year.* New York: First Anchor Books, 2005.

Reichl, Ruth. *Tender at the Bone: Growing Up at the Table.* New York: Random House, 2010.

Rizzo, Steve. *Get Your SHIFT Together: How to Think, Laugh, and Enjoy Your Way to Success in Business and in Life.* New York: McGraw-Hill, 2013.

Gem 6—Illuminating Your Unique Wiring

Aron, Elaine N. *The Highly Sensitive Person.* New York: Broadway Books, 1997.

———. *The Highly Sensitive Person's Workbook.* Broadway Books, 1999.

Hallowell, Edward M., and John J. Ratey. *Delivered from Distraction: Getting the Most Out of Life with Attention Deficit Disorder.* New York: Ballantine, 2005.

Loehr, Jim. *The Power of Full Engagement: Managing Energy, Not Time, Is the Key to High Performance and Personal Renewal.* New York: Free Press, 2003.

Maurer, Robert. *One Small Step Can Change Your Life: The Kaizen Way.* New York: Workman Publishing, 2014.

Moroney, Jean. "Excellent Strategies for Staying Motivated and Goal Completion." *Thinking Directions.* http://www.thinkingdirections.com/sparkle/

Nelson, Portia. *There's a Hole in My Sidewalk: The Romance of Self-Discovery.* Hillsboro, OR: Beyond Words, 1993.

Rubin, Gretchen. *Better Than Before: Mastering the Habits of Everyday Lives.* New York: Crown Publishers, 2015.

Scott, S.J. *Develop Good Habits.* http://www.developgoodhabits.com/

———. *Bad Habits No More: 25 Steps to Break Any Bad Habit.* Oldtown Publishing LLC, 2014.

Scott, S.J., and Rebecca Livermore. *The Daily Entrepreneur: 33 Success Habits for Small Business Owners, Freelancers, and Aspiring 9-to-5 Escape Artists.* CreateSpace Independent Publishing Platform, 2014.

Sher, Barbara. *Refuse to Choose! Use All of Your Interests, Passions, and Hobbies to Create the Life and Career of Your Dreams.* Emmaus, PA: Rodale Books, 2006.

Ward, Karol. *Find Your Inner Voice: Using Instinct and Intuition Through the Body-Mind Connection.* Franklin Lakes, NJ: New Page Books, 2009.

Autonomous Sensory Meridian Response (ASMR) Stress-Reduction Resources

AirLight. YouTube channel. https://www.youtube.com/channel/UC4XtEiJW3LaQeSxktn4Y1OA

The ASMR Report. http://asmrr.org/

"Autonomous Sensory Meridian Response." *Wikipedia.* https://en.wikipedia.org/wiki/Autonomous_sensory_meridian_response

GentleWhispering. YouTube channel. https://www.youtube.com/channel/UC6gLlIAnzg7eJ8VuXDCZ_vg

WhisperCrystal. YouTube channel. https://www.youtube.com/channel/UC2N1l0fHMdcGcvpEJFTvihg

Yang Hai-Ying. YouTube channel. https://www.youtube.com/channel/UCWGJYBUTSmy8Sh3pDqzKRng

Gem 7—Fire Your Perfectionist

Barth, Lois. "Having Fun with Your Itty Bitty Committee." *Smart Sexy TV: What Nobody Talks About... but Everyone Needs to Hear.* YouTube, July 12, 2016. https://youtu.be/3fbdG7KRkIs

———. "Itty Bitty Committee Exercise: Letting Your Negative Self Talk Know Who's In Charge." Smart Sexy TV: What Nobody Talks About... but Everyone Needs to Hear. YouTube, July 12, 2016. https://youtu.be/3XuDJZ4um54

Goodman, Marion. *Addiction to Perfection: The Still Unravished Bride: A Psychological Study.* Toronto, Canada: Inner City Books, 1982.

Spar, Debora L. *Wonder Women*: Sex, Power, and the Quest for Perfection. New York: Sarah Crichton Books, 2013.

Stone, Hal, and Sidra L. Stone. *Embracing Ourselves: The Voice Dialogue* Manual. Novato, CA: Nataraj, 1989.

Gem 8—How to Shine in Your Career

Barth, Lois. "Don't Tap Dance Around Your Power: Learn How to Communicate Powerfully About Who You Are and What You're Up To." *Smart Sexy TV: What Nobody Talks About... but Everyone Needs to Hear*. YouTube, July 12, 2016. *https://youtu.be/-1ObrXE9d7k*

Crowley, Katherine, and Kathi Elster. *Working for You Isn't Working Me: How to Get Ahead When Your Boss Holds You Back*. New York: Portfolio/Penguin, 2009.

———. *Working With You is Killing Me: Freeing Yourself from Emotional Traps at Work*. New York: Warner Business Books, 2006.

Jeffers, Susan. *Feel the Fear...and Do It Anyway*. New York: Ballantine Books, 2006.

Klaus, Peggy. *Brag! The Art of Tooting Your Own Horn Without Blowing It*. New York: Warner Books, 2003.

———. *The Hard Truth About Soft Skills: Workplace Lessons Smart People Wish They'd Learned Sooner*. New York: HarperCollins, 2008.

Lencioni, Patrick. *The Five Dysfunctions of a Team: A Leadership Fable*. San Francisco: Jossey-Bass, 2002.

Moran, Brian P., and Michael Lennington. *The 12 Week Year: Get More Done in 12 Weeks Than Others Do in 12 Months*. Hoboken, NJ: John Wiley & Sons, 2013.

Olson, Jeff. The Slight Edge: The Secret to a Successful Life. Lake Dallas, TX: Success Books, 2005.

Rath, Tom. *StrengthsFinder 2.0.* New York: Gallup Press, 2007.

Riegel, Deborah Grayson, et al. *Money Talks: 100 Strategies to Master Tricky Conversations about Money.* Ridgefield, CT: American BookWorks, 2015.

Sandberg, Sheryl. *Lean In: Women, Work, and the Will to Lead.* New York: Alfred A. Knopf, 2013.

Gem 9—From Dimmers to Shimmers

Barth, Lois. "En-Spiration: Using Envy as a Roadmap to Create a Life That Inspires You." *Smart Sexy TV: What Nobody Talks About... But Everybody Needs to Hear.* YouTube, July 12, 2016. https://youtu.be/IPxjXSZi7fo

———. "Un-trigger Your Stress in Five Minutes or Less." *Smart Sexy TV: What Nobody Talks About... But Everybody Needs to Hear.* YouTube, July 12, 2016. https://youtu.be/iA4vZTJnM1E

Beck, Martha. *The Joy Diet: 10 Daily Practices for a Happier Life.* New York: Crown Publishers, 2003.

Borysenko, Joan. *Why You Burn Out and How to Revive.* Carlsbad, CA: Hay House, 2011.

Chodron, Pema. *When Things Fall Apart: Heart Advice for Difficult Times.* Boston: Shambhala Publications, 1997.

Hallowell, Edward M. *CrazyBusy: Overstretched, Overbooked, and About to Snap! Strategies for Handling Your Fast-Paced Life.* New York: Ballantine Books, 2006.

Huffington, Arianna. *Thrive: The Third Metric to Redefining Success and Creating a Life of Well-Being, Wisdom, and Wonder.* New York: Harmony Books, 2014.

Roth, Geneen. *Breaking Free from Compulsive Eating.* New York: Plume, 1993.

Ward, Karol. *Worried Sick: Break Free from Chronic Worry to Achieve Mental & Physical Health*. New York: Berkley Publishing Group, 2010.

Gem 10—Creating Your Scintillating Circle of Support

Barth, Lois. "The Anatomy of Being Slimed: How to Reboot After Dealing with a Toxic Person." *Smart Sexy TV: What Nobody Talks About...But Everyone Needs to Hear*. YouTube, July 12, 2016. https://youtu.be/-l1fR_JM5RU

Collins, Jim. *Good to Great: Why Some Companies Make the Leap... and Others Don't*. New York: HarperCollins, 2001.

Edut, Ophira, and Tali Edut. *The AstroTwins' Love Zodiac: The Essential Astrology Guide for Women*. Naperville, IL: Sourcebooks Casablanca, 2008.

———. *Momstrology: The AstroTwins' Guide to Parenting Your Little One by the Stars*. New York: HarperCollins, 2014.

Godin, Seth. *Tribes: We Need You to Lead Us*. New York: Portfolio, 2008.

Spaulding, Tommy. *It's Not Just Who You Know: Transform Your Life (and Your Organization) by Turning Colleagues and Contacts into Lasting, Genuine Relationships*. New York: Broadway Books, 2010.

Gem 11—Communication that Glistens

Barth, Lois. "How to Kvetch Responsibly! Learn How to Set Boundaries for Those Well-meaning but Irresponsible Kvetchers." *Smart Sexy TV: What Nobody Talks About... But Everyone Needs to Hear*. YouTube, July 12, 2016. https://youtu.be/WR8uqLqNPz0

Chapman, Gary. *The Five Love Languages: How to Express Heartfelt Commitment to Your Mate*. Chicago: Northfield, 1995.

Gordon, Jon. *The No Complaining Rule: Positive Ways to Deal with Negativity at Work*. Hoboken, NJ: John Wiley & Sons, 2008.

Latz, Jayne. *Communicate Up the Corporate Ladder: How to Succeed in Business with Clarity and Confidence*. Oceanside, CA: Indie Books International, 2016.

Gem 12—The 5Cs of Creating a Life That Lights You Up

Beck, Martha. *Diana, Herself: An Allegory of Awakening*. Arroyo Grande, CA: Cynosure Publishing, 2016.

Damien, Richard. *A Monk in the World: Fully Being Your Spiritual Self in Life*. Lincoln, NE: iUniverse, 2006.

Eddington, Karen C. *Understanding Self Worth*. Brigham City, UT: Brigham Distributing, 2014.

Gershon, David, and Gail Straub. *Empowerment: The Art of Creating Your Life as You Want It*. New York: Sterling, 2011.

Kidd, Sue M. *When the Heart Waits: Spiritual Direction for Life's Sacred Questions*. San Francisco: HarperSanFrancisco, 2006.

Moran, Victoria. *Lit from Within: Tending Your Soul for Lifelong Beauty*. San Francisco: HarperSanFrancisco, 2001.

Ruiz, Don M., and Janet Mills. *The Four Agreements: A Practical Guide to Personal Freedom*. San Rafael, CA: Amber-Allen Publishing, 1997.

Tharp, Twyla. *The Creative Habit: Learn It and Use It for Life*. New York: Simon & Schuster, 2003.

CPSIA information can be obtained at www.ICGtesting.com
Printed in the USA
BVOW01s2313071016

464499BV00008B/11/P